AF521842

AIR COMBAT WITH THE MIGHTY 8TH

A Teenage Warrior In World War II

By

Wm. L. Cramer, Jr.

EAKIN PRESS ★ Austin, Texas

FIRST EDITION

Published in the United States of America
By Eakin Press
An Imprint of Sunbelt Media, Inc.
P.O. Drawer 90159 Austin, TX 78709-0159

ISBN 0-89015-939-4

Dedication

To the youth of today . . . This is just one story of what my generation did for our country and future generations during World War II. We didn't use or even know about drugs. We didn't need them because we got our "highs" flying airplaines and knowing we were serving our country. We only had one "gang," the Army Air Corps. We also felt that you, our future generations, would be worth our sacrifices.

To my wife for over thirty years, Mabel Lawson Cramer. You are the best thing to happen to me, and every day "you light up my life."

To my son, Capt. Alden S. Cramer, USAF. I have always been proud of you, and I'm pleased you took my place in the Air Force.

To my granddaughter, Samantha Cramer. We went all the way to St. Vito, Italy, to see you when you were born; it was worth the trip.

To my grandson, Richie Cramer. You are all boy, so I know you must be enjoying your dad's assignment to Alaska.

To my mother, Helen Winninger Cramer, for teaching me so many things about life and how to be a gentleman, even before I started school. You prepared me well.

To my grandmother, Margaret Boulware Cramer. You gave me a loving home after my mother died and continued her teaching of life. I shall never forget you.

To my uncle, Russell Elton Cramer. You were like a father to me, and I shall always remember you gave me my first new bicycle.

To my aunt, Marie Diskin Cramer. Your laughter always told me you were the one in the Cramer family with a wonderful sense of humor.

To my aunt, Verna Cramer Easton. You helped my grandmother raise me as though I was your own son – but you did spoil me.

To my father, William Lowell Cramer, Sr. I always regretted we did not have a meaningful father-son relationship. However, that made me strive to succeed in everything I did, just to show you I could.

Contents

Acknowledgments vii
1. Basic Training 1
2. Bombardier Training 6
3. Aerial Gunnery School 10
4. Combat Crew Training I 14
5. Combat Crew Training II 22
6. En Route to War 30
7. The Beginning of Air Combat 37
8. A Pause in My War 42
9. Rejoining the Fight 49
10. After D-Day 65
11. Second Combat Tour 85
12. "Breakfast at three, briefing at four!" 96
13. Prisoner of War 103
14. The Escape 109
15. Home at Last 121
16. My Quest 132
William L. Cramer, Jr., Post World War II 149
Index 155

Acknowledgments

I would like to express my appreciation to many friends and associates for their kind criticism and guidance as I wrote this, my first book. Since this is an autobiography, I knew more about the subject than anyone else but did not know how best to relate the story to others. Tom Wilcox, a fellow evader and author of his own story, *One Man's Destiny,* took the time to edit completely and provide suggestions. Reading Tom's book inspired me to write my own.

At weekly readings before fellow members of the Trinity Arts Writers' Associates (TAWA), their critiques and suggestions were very valuable. Jack Fryrear and Jeff Buehner, who edited my manuscript from beginning to end, provided very worthwhile assistance.

Dr. David MacKena, my department head when I was teaching at the University of Texas at Arlington, provided invaluable editing and counsel.

My brother-in-law, Buford Lawson, a former B-17 crew member, and now head of Lawson & Associates, Design/Art/Production, designed the cover for the book.

Zoot suit in 1941.

CHAPTER 1

Basic Training

It was December 8, 1941, the day after the Japanese attack on Pearl Harbor. Like so many youths my age, I was full of patriotism. I decided to enlist in the Army Air Corps to fight for my country.

After waiting in line at the U.S. Army Enlistment Office for six and a half hours, I finally got to the head of the line. The sergeant said, "How old are you, son?"

"Almost eighteen, sir, and I'm ready to fight for my country."

"I'm sorry, son, but the law says you have to be eighteen. Come back then and I'll be glad to sign you up."

On my eighteenth birthday, May 2, 1942, I decided that this was to be the day my adventure would start. My good friend Johnny Meents (still a good friend today, after fifty years) walked with me to the streetcar that would take me to the downtown area of Cincinnati so that I could enlist in the Army Air Corps. Standing there with one foot on the step of the streetcar, and with the motorman glaring at me for holding him up, Johnny and I shook hands and he told me, "Go get 'em, tiger!"

How naive I must have sounded when I asked the recruiting sergeant, "Sir, if I enlist, can I fly airplanes?" Of course, his reply was, "Son, if you enlist, you can do anything you want to do." I enlisted as Pvt. William L. Cramer, Jr.

After going through the enlistment physical and signing all my enlistment papers, I was told to take the papers home for my father to sign. On the way home I stopped at the house where my sister was living and told her, "I've enlisted in the Army Air Corps, and I'll be leaving tomorrow for Ft. Thomas." She did not appear to be the least bit surprised.

At home I told my father, "My enlistment papers need your signature." He probably thought I was joking because he signed the papers without asking me any questions. Actually, he never asked me questions about anything, so that was about what I expected. My mother and he were divorced when I was just three years old. My newborn sister, Betty Jane, and I lived with our mother until she died when I was twelve and Betty was nine.

After our mother's death, I was reared by my wonderful Grandmother Cramer. My sister was taken in first by our mother's dearest friend and later by another friend of the family. I was never able to understand why Betty and I could not have been brought up together. We used to have our arguments, as do most brothers and sisters, but nothing serious. I have always had a deep-seated resentment toward my father for allowing that separation to happen. My lack of a relationship with my father was probably the motivating force that caused me to strive so hard to succeed at everything I undertook. The Army gave me the chance to show the world that I didn't need my father's help to be a winner.

I did not get to see much of my father during my childhood because he was always too busy with his girlfriends. It's a terrible thing to realize, but my father never bought me so much as a pocketknife. And I had to get my first adult friend, George Runte, to teach me to drive an automobile when I was fifteen. The next summer George hired me to use his auto to make small package deliveries for his hardware store. He always allowed me time off to play baseball.

After processing at Ft. Thomas, I was sent to Keesler Field, Mississippi, for the Army General Classification Test, math test, and a whole battery of other tests so that the Army could determine for what I was best suited. The testing process seemed quite easy for me, since I had been in school from age five until the day I enlisted. By the time I was four, my mother had already taught me simple spelling, math, and reading.

I scored 141 on the AGCT (Army General Classification Test), which qualified me for any technical school and any branch of the Army. (In later years, that 141 AGCT score also qualified me for membership in MENSA, the international high I.Q. society.)

The sergeant in personnel said that I had to name two choices. I requested the Aviation Cadet Program or Paratroopers, but it was necessary for me to complete basic training before going to any other school.

Basic training in Mississippi, during May and June, was just plain miserable. We were housed in Tent City, eight men to a tent, and it rained every night and almost every day. Of course, we were not allowed off base, so for excitement we would buy marshmallows in the post exchange and then have marshmallow box races. We floated the boxes out of our tent in the steady stream of water that was always present. Mosquitoes out there had stingers that seemed longer than the needles the medics used for our numerous shots. Those mosquitoes were so big, they could have carried off the marshmallows if we hadn't kept them covered.

We began our basic training with regular drilling, gas mask training, the obstacle course, long hikes with full field packs, and drilling in various formations. Of course, there was always guard duty on the muddy roads in the pitch black rainy night of Tent City, with only a flashlight and a night stick.

At the end of our second week of basic training, the first sergeant called me into the Orderly Room and told me that since I had ROTC before enlisting, my new job would be as an assistant drill instructor. I was to wear a single arm band with the rank of acting corporal, but my pay would still be that of a private—$21 a month. At the end of my first month, I owed the government $7 because it was too easy to just sign for the many PX chits, laundry chits, and theater chits. I asked the flight sergeant if they could take it out of my next pay because we had been informed that a private's pay was going up then to $50. His reply was, "You owe the government $7, send home for the money." I never did send home for the money, and the $7 was duly deducted from my pay for June.

Corporal Rueban was our DI (drill instructor), and he had been up and down the promotion ladder numerous times. He made it to staff sergeant one time, but he was always getting busted because he got drunk every payday. Corporal Rueban was only 5'4 and probably didn't weigh much over 120 pounds, but he was in good shape, tough as nails, and an excellent DI. I felt very fortunate to have been appointed his assistant. However, I was concerned about how my friends in the flight would react. They all told me, "You've been doing the drilling whenever Corporal Rueban is 'under the weather,' so you *should* be the assistant DI."

The second week in my new job, I saw firsthand that when the Army made a mistake, it was not admitted. There was a sergeant vacancy in our flight and instead of Corporal Rueban being promoted, orders were posted on the bulletin board announcing, for all to see, that Pvt. William L. Cramer, Jr., was promoted to sergeant. I was on KP at the time, and four of my tentmates ran over to the mess hall to tell me about my promotion. I thought they were joking, as we were always playing tricks on each other. But when I got off KP and went to the bulletin board, there it was. I then went to the Orderly Room and said to the first sergeant, "Somebody must have made a mistake." He let me know, in very specific terms, that the Army never makes mistakes. Corporal Rueban must have heard about the "non-mistake" because he took off. I heard later that he stayed drunk for a month. At just barely eighteen years of age, I became the drill instructor for our flight until we graduated from basic training.

A week after being promoted to sergeant, I was called into the Orderly Room and was informed that my request for the Cadet Training Program had been approved. However, the only opening was for Bombardier School. That didn't matter to me—as long as I could fly.

Army of the United States

To all who shall see these presents, greeting:

Know ye, that reposing special trust and confidence in the fidelity and abilities of Private WILLIAM L. CRAMER, JR., I do hereby appoint him * Sergeant (temporary) AAFU, ARMY OF THE UNITED STATES, to rank as such from the eighteenth day of June one thousand nine hundred and forty-two He is therefore carefully and diligently to discharge the duty of † Sergeant by doing and performing all manner of things thereunto belonging. And I do strictly charge and require all Noncommissioned Officers and Soldiers under his command to be obedient to his orders as Sergeant. And he is to observe and follow such orders and directions from time to time, as he shall receive from his Superior Officers and Noncommissioned Officers set over him, according to the rules and discipline of War.

Given under my hand at Keesler Field, Mississippi this eigtheenth day of June in the year of our Lord one thousand nine hundred and forty-two

Henry H. Hunter

HENRY H. HUNTER, Captain, Air Corps, Commandant of Students

W. D., A. G. O. Form No. 58
March 25, 1921

* Insert grade, company, and regiment or arm or service; e. g., "Corporal, Company A, 1st Infantry," "Sergeant, Quartermaster Corps."
† Insert grade.

10—22076

CHAPTER 2

Bombardier Training

Upon graduation from basic training, my next assignment was to Buckley Field in Denver, Colorado, for bombardier training. As a sergeant, I became an aviation student and wore the cadet patch with a black background instead of blue, in addition to the large wing and prop hat insignia worn by the others. I was the youngest of the five aviation students in my flight.

We were all very excited about flying, even though we acted very blasé. We had several weeks of ground school, however, before we even got close to an airplane.

Hazing was continuous for aviation students. In our flight, all of the upper classmen had entered the Cadet Program directly from civilian life, and they seemed to take a fiendish delight in hazing all of us – especially the aviation students. When they found out that I had entered the Cadet Program as a sergeant with only two months of service, I was singled out for special treatment.

Whenever I met an upper classman, he would put me in a brace (made to stand at rigid attention) and tell me, "Tuck in your gut, mister, and make chins . . . I said *make chins!*" After so much of that, I began to laugh at them and, as expected, I was assigned demerits for each infraction. When ten demerits were "earned," that meant walking a four-hour punishment tour wearing a seat pack parachute and a helmet with goggles over your eyes. My tactical officer told me, just before I graduated, "You have set an unenviable record of walking more punishment tours than any cadet prior to your time."

In ground school we were taught the composition and operation of the Norden bombsight, the bombardier's instrument panel, the proper loading of different types of bombs in the bomb bay, how to install and remove the bombsight from different types of aircraft, and great emphasis was placed on security for the bombsight. We were also taught how to be gentlemen, how to use military courtesy and protocol, how to use the proper utensils at a dinner table, ad finitum. Most of the latter lessons my mother taught me before I started to school.

Our flying started in the AT-6. Probably the only reason for that was to see how many would have to be washed out for getting airsick—and there were quite a few. They really put us through the whole acrobatic menu. The maneuver that almost got me was called the "hammer head stall." The instructor pulled the stick back into his lap and climbed straight up until the aircraft stalled, seemed to stop in midair, then violently did a wingover and dived straight down. The maneuver most likely was so named because it felt like someone had hit you in the head with a hammer.

When our serious flying and dropping bombs started, it was my good fortune to be assigned to a group of cadets who were to take flight training in a B-34. The bombsight was a Norden, and the instrument panel was the same as was used in ground school.

The big day had come. We marched out to the aircraft for our first practice bomb drops. All ten of us in the flight thought we were real hot shots as we all talked about getting a "shack" (dropping our bomb on the wooden shack in the middle of the bombing circle). Since we were taking turns in alphabetical order, I was to be number four to take my position at the bombsight in the nose of the aircraft. We were each to drop three 100-pound bombs from an 8,000-foot altitude. The bomb dropped closest to the target would be our score for the day. With three cadets to drop ahead of me, I used the time to study my notes and my textbook on the Norden bombsight.

Finally, it was my turn to take a position in the nose. Our bomb run was very smooth that day. Bending over the bombsight to line up the target with the cross hairs, I opened the bomb bay doors and kept backing off the cross hairs until we reached the aiming point that I had figured would give me a good score. The cross hairs merged and the bomb dropped. I closed the bomb bay doors and began making calculations for my next drop, as we would be coming into the target area from a different heading. A lot of yelling arose from the rear of the plane, and one of my friends came up to the nose of the aircraft, shouting, "You just blew the hell out of the building in the middle of the bombing circle!" I got a shack with the first bomb that I ever dropped. There was no way to get any better score, so I did not have to drop any more bombs that day.

As difficult as it is to admit, the first bomb that I ever dropped was my best score. I never did get another shack during Bombardier School training. But I *was* the only one in my class who did.

Graduation day arrived. We all stood at attention in formation, dressed in our "pinks and greens" (Class A uniform for Army officers). We did not have to pay the tailor downtown for them until we received our initial uniform allowance of $200. The commandant of cadets passed down the line and stopped in front of each cadet, pinned on the silver wings of a bombardier, and handed the cadet a card with two gold bars and two U.S. and wing and prop lapel insignia before shaking his hand. When the commandant stopped in front of me, he pinned on my bombardier wings, shook my hand, and said, "Sergeant Cramer, I regret to inform you that you are too young to be commissioned." He was about three men beyond me before the shock of what he had said hit me between the eyes.

Unfortunately, this happened before the flight officer rating (which did not require twenty-one years of age) was authorized. So, after putting up with all of that crap and hazing, Sgt. Bill Cramer graduated from the Cadet Program with the same rank he had upon entering the program. I felt that I had been betrayed by the Army.

Never in my life have I been more bitter about anything. I was devastated. After the formation broke up, I tore my bombardier wings off my new green officer's blouse and threw them as far as I could. I could taste the awful bitterness in my mouth, like bile bubbling up from my stomach. My friends all tried to console me, but nothing they said did any good. One of my friends who received his commission did agree to take the $200 worth of uniforms off my hands.

I went to the barracks and changed into my GI uniform with the sergeant stripes and then went to the Orderly Room to see Cpl. Al Fritz, a friend of mine from basic training and at that time the special orders clerk for the Bombardier School. When he asked me what happened to my wings, I told him what had occurred.

He was very surprised. “You graduated number-two in your class, and I have been instructed to put you and two others, who also scored well, on orders as instructors at the Bombardier School,” he said.

I told Al, “If you don’t put me on orders immediately to go to Aerial Gunnery School, I’ll go AWOL.”

Of course, we would both have faced a court-martial if we had been caught. Nevertheless, I shipped out the next day for Aerial Gunnery School at Tyndall Field in Panama City, Florida.

CHAPTER 3

Aerial Gunnery School

All of the other students in the class were privates, with the exception of four who were corporals and one sergeant – me. Still riddled with bitterness, Sgt. Bill Cramer was appointed flight sergeant. As soon as our ground school started, I got busy because being number-one in my class was so important to my morale. I still refused to wear my bombardier wings or even tell anyone that I was a trained bombardier.

During our four weeks of intense ground school training, we learned the operation and dismantling of air-cooled machine guns and various turrets. We had classes in aircraft recognition (so we wouldn't shoot down our own fighter planes), skeet shooting (to learn how to lead a target), and hazards of high-altitude flying. Apparently exhibiting a knack for weapons, I was assigned to special classes and became a weapons specialist. Upon graduation, my rating was changed to armour/gunner.

Our air-to-air gunnery training at Tyndall Field started by using a .30-caliber machine gun, mounted in the back of an AT-6, to fire at targets being towed by another AT-6. We were then sent to Apalachicola for our last week of air-to-air gunnery. During that period of my training, I met and flew with several pilots who were sergeants and staff sergeants. I later learned there were many "flying sergeants" in the Air Corps. Those men were excellent pilots, but, for reasons I never learned, they could not qualify for a commission. At least they were informed beforehand that they would not be commissioned. To this day, I cannot understand why I was not informed that I was too young to be commissioned before I entered the Cadet Program. I could have accepted that, and certainly would have gone through the program anyhow. Because I was not informed, I felt betrayed by the Army.

Meeting and flying with those "flying sergeants" helped ease some of my disappointment, and I began feeling better. However, I still was not ready to talk about being trained as a bombardier, and I was more determined than ever to finish number-one in my class.

After returning to Tyndall, we had one more ground school class on aircraft recognition and then graduation. That graduation was quite different from my previous one. All of the privates and corporals were promoted to sergeant (three stripes). Because I graduated first in my class, I was promoted to staff sergeant (three stripes and a rocker). The base Public Information Office and U.S. Army Recruiting made a big deal out of my being the youngest staff sergeant in the Army Air Corps.

As the school commandant moved down our formation and pinned on our wings, the first sergeant whispered to me, "The old man wants to see you after the formation."

When I headed for the commandant's office, I had a sinking feeling in the pit of my stomach. Had I done something wrong? Was I going to get screwed again by the Army? Instead, I was in for a pleasant surprise. Four other recently graduated gunners were in the room. The commandant advised us, "Lt. Clark Gable, the movie star, and his cameraman, Lt. Andy McIntyre, are coming to Tyndall to take a hurry-up class in aerial gunnery and you men have been selected to be their instructors. They will be your only students, and the class will be four weeks long. Upon completion, all five of you will have your choice of any type of combat bomber and any overseas command."

What a relief! I wasn't in trouble, and after four weeks I would be on my way to the 8th Air Force and combat in a B-17. Even though some bomb groups in the 8th Air Force were experiencing 100 percent losses, I had joined the Army to fight, and that's where I wanted to be—not in the rear ranks.

We had only three days to modify the course of instruction for a special abbreviated aerial gunnery class. We were sure that we would have all of the assistance we needed from the school staff and the other instructors. Although the other class instructors were understandably envious of our assignment, they could not have been more helpful, especially in designing a special curriculum for that short course.

Later in the day, the commandant brought Lieutenants Gable and McIntyre to the main classroom, introduced all of us, and departed. At first we were in complete awe just from being in the same room with Clark Gable. He put us all at ease with a smile and said, "Tell us what you're going to tell us." He was referring to the Army training method: tell them what you're going to tell them, tell them, then tell them what you told them. We all laughed. Then we briefed them on what part each of us would handle in their training. Lieutenant Gable asked, "Will we do any skeet shooting?" Since I was the weapons instructor, I told him, "We'll have four days of small arms training, which will include skeet shooting." That brought out the Clark Gable smile again, and we all began to feel very comfortable with him and Andy.

After the briefing, Lieutenant Gable wanted to go to the PX to buy some shirts and I offered to show him the way. We entered the PX and went to the back of the store, where military clothing was located. When we walked up to the counter, the salesgirl was bent over the counter, looking at some invoices. When she raised up, her face was just six inches from the face of Clark Gable. Her mouth flew open, she gasped something, and wet her pants. It was obvious because a puddle ran out from under the counter. Lieutenant Gable was every bit the gentleman and pretended not to notice, but he did move his feet a little to the side. He bought three new uniform shirts and we departed. As we left the PX, he said, "I felt so sorry for that young lady."

That incident was indicative of the type of fine gentleman that Clark Gable was during the time I knew him. It bothers me to this day that I never asked him for his autograph. It just never entered my mind.

The first day on the skeet range, using GI shotguns, Lieutenant Gable missed two or three clay pigeons each round. But on the next two days of shooting, he did not miss a single bird. In fact, he set a range record for breaking the most consecutive birds. He told me later, "I guess you know that during lunch on our first day of skeet shooting, I called California and had a friend send my special skeet gun by air." I told him that I kind of suspected that. He never did say how the gun got there the next day. It wouldn't surprise me if he had his friend charter a plane just to fly his gun to him.

The four weeks to train our special students went by very quickly. We instructors drew straws, and I won the honor of pinning on Lieutenant Gable's aerial gunner wings. While having coffee later, he told me that he and Andy had orders sending them to photography school and then to the 8th Air Force to make a movie of bomber crews in combat. All five of the instructors chipped in and threw a going away party for Lieutenants Gable and McIntyre the night before they departed.

We did not have long to wait for our promised reward. We were called into the Orderly Room individually to choose our next assignments. I chose B-17s in the European Theater of Operations, which I knew meant the 8th Air Force. That's where the air combat was, and that's where I wanted to be.

RAPID PROMOTION

Here's cheering news for those 18 and 19-year-olds facing induction who fear that an Army career is a tediously slow process! Staff Sergt. W. L. Cramer, son of Mr. and Mrs. W. Cramer, 2827 Astoria street, has been a private, private first class, corporal, sergeant and staff sergeant since he became a part of the Army five months ago. Sergt. Cramer is stationed at the Army Air Forces' Flexible Gunnery School, Tyndall Field, Fla.

* * *

New S/Sgt. Armour Gunner

CHAPTER 4

Combat Crew Training I

My special orders were handed to me in the mess hall while we "Clark Gable" instructors were having breakfast. They assigned me to the OTU (Overseas Training Unit) at Sioux City Army Air Base in Iowa. That particular OTU had B-17s and was the departure point for combat crews going to England and the 8th Air Force. It began to look like my reason for enlisting was about to be fulfilled. I was finally on my way to combat. The other four special instructors still had not received their orders, so I went back to the barracks to complete my packing.

There were only a few things left to toss into my duffle bag, as I had done most of my packing right after I made my request. Guess I was naive enough to be willing to trust the Army to keep its promise to me one more time—but I still refused to wear bombardier wings.

Our group of newly graduated aerial gunners loaded into seven 2½-ton trucks and headed for the troop train in Panama City that would take us to Sioux City, Iowa. None of us expected a vacation type of train trip, but neither did we anticipate such a long, horrible ride.

The original departure time of 1500 hours was delayed for three hours. As usual, it was hurry up and wait. We were loaded onto the train two hours before the planned departure time. It was a steamy hot October in Florida, and no one had yet thought about air conditioning trains. We finally were pulled out of the station by a big steam engine that belched smoke and hot ashes into our open windows, making it difficult to see or breathe.

At that point in my life, I had never spent a more miserable eight days as on that trip to Iowa. The train took us from Panama

City to Atlanta, Memphis, Louisville, Cincinnati, Chicago, Minneapolis, and finally, Sioux City. During our entire eight-day trip, there was no place for anyone to take a shower and, with over 300 men on that troop train, shaving facilities were very limited. The lack of shaving did not bother me too much, as I only had to shave once every week or ten days. But the lack of a shower bothered all of us. It caused our day coach to smell worse than a cattle feed lot.

There were poker games in the baggage car and crap games all over the train, even though gambling was strictly taboo. I played a little and won a little, but some of the guys lost everything they owned. Alcohol was also prohibited, but everyone who wanted a bottle seemed to have one. I drank too much Jack Daniels with some friends the third night of our trip and I had never been so sick as on the morning after, probably because of the rocking of the train. However, I was not alone.

The troop train took us onto the Sioux City Army Air Base. We then had to go through processing before we could go to the barracks for a shave, shower, and clean clothes. I really felt sorry for the permanent party people who had to process that foul-smelling bunch into the OTU. Probably because of our pitiful and smelly condition, it was quickly decided that we would be assigned to barracks and that OTU processing would take place the following day.

Once in the barracks, I peeled down to what I was born with, threw away the underwear and socks I had been wearing for eight days, and hit the shower. I think I stayed in the shower for more than an hour. I can't remember when a simple thing like that shower gave me a more refreshed feeling. I put on a clean uniform with my new gunner's wings and went to the Orderly Room to see if I could get a pass for town. Soon I was on the bus with a lot of other GIs, heading for the big city.

When we arrived, I got off the bus and started walking. After being packed into a troop train with over 300 GIs for eight days, I just wanted to be alone for a while. The smell of burning leaves reminded me that this would be the time of the year for football practice back home. I suddenly remembered the year my football playing was cut short by a broken nose and four broken fingers on my right hand. I also remembered Patty, Roberta and Connie, fraternity and sorority dances, final exams . . .

I found myself in front of a "mom and pop" type of restaurant. It looked and smelled good, so I went in. The hamburger, french fries, cold milk, and homemade cherry pie I had were delicious—exactly the same thing I would have ordered at the Purple Cow back in good old Cincinnati. Afterwards, more exercise seemed like a good idea because I felt stuffed. After about an hour of walking, the local USO Club loomed up in front of me. I found four friends inside, and we decided to play some pool until the dance started.

When we heard the band playing "In the Mood," we racked our pool cues and headed for the ballroom. A large dance band was playing Glenn Miller-type music, and they were good. My friends quickly found dancing partners; I opted to stand around for a while, looking over the pretty local girls. I soon spotted a young lady with black hair and green eyes sitting at a table. The last time I had scanned that area she had been sitting with three other young ladies. Since she was now alone, I went over to the table and introduced myself. She invited me to sit down.

Her name was Jean, she lived with her parents, and she worked in a department store in Sioux City. We had a Coke, and then I asked her if she would like to dance. The medley of Glenn Miller tunes—"String of Pearls," "Deep Purple," and "Tuxedo Junction"—caused my thoughts to flash back to dances with the same songs back home, in spite of my pretty dancing partner.

Back at the table, Jean's three friends and their dates had returned, so we pulled up some more chairs and everyone introduced themselves. I was the only one at the table wearing wings, and I noticed all of the girls staring at them.

Jean and I danced until closing time. I really enjoyed her company. Before leaving, I asked her for a date, and she told me that it was a serious violation of USO Club rules for the girls to make dates at the Club. However, she did give me her parents' home phone number. It appeared we had developed an interest in each other.

The next day our processing was completed and we were assigned to combat crews and an aircraft. But first we had to attend ground school for a week, and then mix in some practice missions so that we could apply what we were learning in ground school. Since I held the dual rating of armour/gunner, I was assigned to the nose gun of the aircraft, in the bombardier position, because we did not yet have a bombardier on the crew. What a strange twist of fate. Of all the men on our crew, only the pilot and navigator had known each other before being assigned to the crew.

With the rush of training that included flying three practice missions, ten days flew by before I had a chance to call Jean. Thinking she would probably not remember me, I almost didn't call. But I did finally call, and she did remember me. She said, "We would like to have you come out to the house for Sunday dinner, if you can get away." For a home-cooked meal, you bet I could get away! Jean gave me her address, told me what bus to take, and instructed me to get off at a little old Greek restaurant. She would meet me there, as it was only a block from her house.

Sunday arrived and I skipped breakfast so that I would be good and hungry for my first home-cooked meal since leaving home about five months earlier. There was a candy shop near the place I had to transfer buses, so I went inside and bought a box of candy for Jean and one for her mother. After all, her mother was fixing me a home-cooked meal.

Jean was waiting for me at the Greek restaurant.

"Did you have any trouble with my directions?" she asked.

"Your directions were perfect. You'd make a good navigator," I told her.

We walked the short distance to her house, where I would spend a pleasant afternoon with Jean and her parents. The meal consisted of steak, baked potato, English peas, a big salad, and cherry pie ala mode for dessert. Jean's dad asked me, "Better than mess hall food?" I told him the food in the air crew mess was not too bad, even though it couldn't come close to this wonderful meal.

I learned that Jean's father had served in the Army in World War I and had been gassed in France but had completely recovered. I also learned that her brother was currently at sea in the Pacific with the Navy. After dinner, we played penny poker and I won three dollars. I know Jean's father folded a couple of times, just so I would win.

Too soon it was time for me to leave, as I had a very early training mission in the morning. I thanked everyone for a most enjoyable day, and I especially thanked Jean's mother for the delicious Sunday dinner. The mother, not Jean, said, "Can you have dinner with us again next Sunday?" I accepted.

I walked to the Greek restaurant and went inside to have a cup of coffee while waiting for my bus. After the owner and I introduced ourselves, we had a friendly chat while he made coffee in the largest coffee urn I had ever seen. When he had everything ready to go, he broke two eggs and tossed them, shells and all, onto the freshly ground coffee. After that he replaced the lid and turned on the switch. He explained, "Greeks always make coffee that way to remove the bitterness." He convinced me – I had never tasted better coffee. I drank three cups with him before my bus arrived, and he refused to let me pay. As I was going out the door, he winked and invited me to stop in any time I was in the area. I'm sure he had seen Jean meet me at the bus stop earlier in the day.

Our next practice mission was scrubbed because of foul weather, so I went over to the bomb trainer to pass some time. The bombing instructor allowed me to climb up on the trainer and make five practice bomb runs. My scores were really good.

"Are you a trained bombardier?" the instructor asked.

I lied. "No, I just find the techniques interesting." I don't know why I went to the bomb trainer, except maybe I wanted to prove to myself that I was still a damn good bombardier.

The weather cleared the next day and our practice navigation and gunnery mission was rescheduled. This was to be a three-ship mission but not in formation; each crew was to apply their own training. The three aircraft were parked next to each other as we did our engine run-ups and pre-flight checks. After we all had started our engines, one of the gunners in the ship next to us got out of his aircraft to retrieve something he had forgotten to put on board. I was in the nose of our aircraft and I watched as he walked toward the spinning propeller of his number-two engine. I screamed at him, but he could not hear me because of the noise of our four engines. Frustrated that I could not make him hear me, I just put my head in my hands and cried. I couldn't bear to watch as he walked into that spinning prop. It took off his head and most of his upper torso. That was the first time I had ever witnessed death.

Although it seemed almost inhuman to continue the mission that day, the powers that be decided it would be best to get us up in the air. Two aircraft took off; I don't know if the dead gunner's crew flew that day or not. When we returned from our practice mission, we learned that the dead gunner's parents had arrived for a surprise visit with him at about the time he walked into that propeller.

Our next mission was a long flight. I was in the radio room when we were cleared to land much sooner than I had expected, so I stayed there and braced myself for the landing.

Just as we touched down, the drag link on the right landing gear broke, the gear collapsed, and we went into a violent ground loop off the right side of the runway. The force of the crash threw me head first through the door that led from the radio room into the bomb bay, and I landed up against the bomb rack. I must have opened my mouth to yell when I went through the door and hit the vertical bomb racks head first, because it took out all of my upper teeth and gums but not my lips or lower teeth. I was out cold when the medics picked me up and took me to the hospital.

The doctors kept me doped up for a couple of days. When I finally regained my senses, a young dental surgeon very proudly put my new teeth in my mouth. He handed me a mirror and pointed out two of the teeth that he made a little crooked so they would look natural. He was so proud of his work that I didn't have the heart to tell him I used to win prizes in grade school for having straight white teeth.

The medic who picked me up at the crash site came by to see me later in the day. He told me, "When I pulled you out of the aircraft, I could tell all of your upper teeth were gone except one that was just hanging by skin. So I reached in and pulled it out to make it even."

Jean found out about the crash from one of her girlfriends who was dating a doctor at the hospital. She came out to see me two days before I was to be discharged from the hospital and invited me to dinner on Sunday. She also told me that her brother, Jack, was home on leave from the Navy.

When Sunday came around, I headed to Jean's house for another home-cooked meal. I met Jack and he seemed like a nice guy, even if he was in the Navy. He later said the same thing about me – even if I was in the Army.

As we sat down to dinner I saw that Jean's mother had thoughtfully prepared all soft food, not knowing that I was doing just fine with my new teeth. As I seasoned my mashed potatoes, some pepper got up my nose and I knew that I was going to sneeze. I reached for my handkerchief but could not get the pocket flap unbuttoned before the sneeze hit. At least my head was turned away from the table before the *ahhh-choo!* My new teeth exploded from my mouth and went flying across the room, landing on the floor.

The room became very quiet. The only thing for me to do was to go over and pick them up, take them to the kitchen, wash them off, put them back in my mouth, and return to the table. Which is exactly what I did. When I walked back into the dining room, everyone was trying to act as though nothing had happened. I looked at Jack and could see he was about to burst, so I winked at him and he let out a roar. We all had a good laugh as I did my best to keep them from coming out again.

When I got ready to leave, Jean asked when I could come back to dinner again.

"My crew finished their training while I was in the hospital and they are leaving for overseas tomorrow. I expect to be assigned to another crew here or to be transferred to another training base within the next couple of days," I told her.

She began to cry, giving me the uneasy feeling that she was starting to get too serious. I told her how much I had enjoyed our time together, but I knew that I was due to go into combat and did not feel it was wise to make any commitments at that time. I said that I would call her when I learned my status.

Jack walked me down to the restaurant. We went inside the restaurant and had a great cup of coffee while waiting for my bus. Learning that Jack had been in some heavy combat with the Navy in the Pacific area, I asked him if he had ever been afraid. He said he was scared when they were under their first air attack, but his chief told him to just decide that he was already dead and the fear would go away. Jack said, "It worked for me." I decided at that moment to do the same thing. From that point on, I felt that I was indestructible and would survive the war, regardless of what happened to me in combat.

I told Jack about my conversation with Jean and that I felt she was starting to get too serious. He said that, judging from her conversation around the house, he knew she was getting serious. Being a combat veteran, he agreed with me about not making any commitments, since I was headed overseas for combat flying. When my bus arrived, I thanked Jack, wished him luck, and headed for the base.

After going through so much training with my crew, it was with a heavy heart that I watched them take off into the wild blue yonder. My new orders transferred me to Plant Park, just outside of Tampa, to be processed for combat crew training.

I telephoned Jean and broke the news. During our long talk she cried and said she would wait for me. I told her I thought she should go on with her life and, when I got back from the war, I would come to see her again and we could decide then what we wanted to do in peacetime.

CHAPTER 5

Combat Crew Training II

On my first day at Plant Park, I was in the snack bar by myself when a fellow came over to the table and introduced himself to me. His name was Paul Quinn, a pilot and a first lieutenant. Paul said he had noticed my staff sergeant stripes and my gunner wings and felt that I must have had some experience. We both had a good laugh when I said, "I was thinking the same about you." He wanted to get a crew together and proposed a very interesting idea: "I'll pick the officers and you pick the enlisted men and we'll form our own combat crew." That sounded good to me, so we decided to start at the first formation in the morning. We would pick our men and then meet for lunch.

At lunch, Paul said, "I've picked out a navigator."

"I picked out a top-notch radio operator and engineer and they are going to help me pick out four high-scoring gunners," I replied.

That afternoon Paul asked, "How about taking an armament class for me? I've got a heavy date in town." I had been excused from all ground school classes because I had completed them in Sioux City before our crash landing. I agreed to take Paul's class. It was easy to do, since all present wore their flying suits and most without any rank. I signed in for him that afternoon and we got 100 percent on his test. All told, I took seven classes for Paul and we never got below a 94 percent on the tests. None of the classes I took for Paul had anything to do with the operation of a B-17 or combat tactics. He was happy with my substituting for him because he got to spend a lot of time with his girlfriend and also did well in ground school.

In addition to taking classes for Paul, I spent most of my spare time at the bomb trainer. The bomb trainer instructor, T/Sgt. Nye, and I had become pretty good friends. As my scores kept improving, he asked me suddenly where I went to Bombardier School. Without thinking, I said Buckley. That was the end of the questioning.

As I was leaving the bomb trainer after what was to be my last session, I had a real shock. I met Paul walking by and he asked me what I was doing in the bomb trainer. I said I was visiting a friend and all Paul said was, "Sure." I suspect that he had reviewed my military records, found I was a trained bombardier, and was waiting for me to tell him why I wore gunner instead of bombardier wings. We went to the PX, where we met the men we had already selected, and got some hamburgers and milkshakes.

That night Paul and I went into Tampa. Paul had a date and I wanted to have a good meal at the Floridian Hotel and be alone with my thoughts about where I was headed. I had an overnight pass and got a room at the hotel.

After putting my bag in the room, I went down to the bar to have a drink before dinner. Even though I was only nineteen years old, no one ever asked a serviceman in uniform how old he was. The piano player at the bar entertained with Hoagy Carmichael tunes. As I listened to the music, an older gentleman in civilian clothes sat down next to me, stuck out his hand, and said, "I'm Hoke Diaz."

I shook his hand and said, "I'm Bill Cramer."

Hoke spoke with a New York accent and we both agreed on how much we enjoyed Hoagy Carmichael's style of music. He bought me another drink and then invited me to have dinner with him and his wife. I thanked him and accepted, then bought him a drink while I nursed the one I had. After a short while he went upstairs to get his wife while I finished my drink.

As I was leaving the bar, Hoke and his wife were just getting off the elevator and he introduced me to his lovely wife. When we went into the restaurant it was evident that everyone knew Hoke Diaz; even the chef came out of the kitchen to greet him. After a delicious dinner, which began with a huge shrimp cocktail and ended with French pastries, we were having our after-dinner coffee when I asked Mrs. Diaz if she minded if I smoked a cigar. She very pleasantly said, "Of course not, but thank you for asking." I pulled out a couple of Tampa Nuggets and offered one to Hoke,

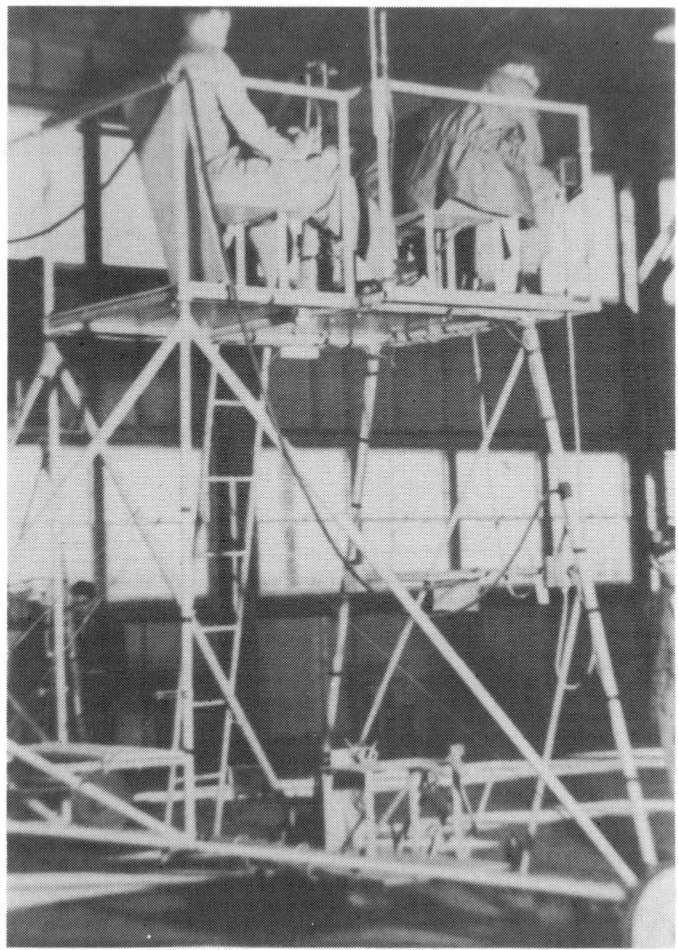

Bombardier trainer

but he declined. He asked me if I had been smoking cigars very long. I admitted that I used to enjoy an occasional pipe, but after I became a sergeant and men the age of my father were coming to me for passes, I reasoned that smoking cigars would make me look older. He smiled, pulled out a leather cigar case, and invited me to try one of his favorites. I looked at the wrapper and all it said was Tampa Diplomat. It was the finest cigar I had ever smoked.

As Hoke was talking with one of the waiters, Mrs. Diaz told me, "Hoke came rushing into our room and told me that he had met a flyer in the bar that reminded him very much of our only son, an Army flyer who was killed at Pearl Harbor. I can also see the resemblance, but our son was about five years older than you."

While I was thanking Hoke for a most enjoyable evening, he handed me the other four cigars from his cigar case and told me to enjoy them. Hoke told me that he and his wife would be in the hotel for another week and to be sure to call them if I came into town again.

Two days later, I had another pass to town. I got there early in the afternoon and, since I had smoked all the fine cigars that Hoke had given me, I thought I would buy some more.

I stopped by a drug store and asked for a box of Tampa Diplomats. The clerk said, "The only place you can buy that type of cigar is at a wholesale tobacco dealer." He gave me an address for one nearby. It was a nice day, so I walked to the wholesale store and asked for a box of Tampa Diplomats. The clerk asked, "Would you like a box of twenty-five or fifty?" Since it was payday, I decided to go all out. I asked for a box of fifty. The Tampa Nuggets I had been smoking were two for five cents, so I expected the Tampa Diplomats would be a little more, perhaps even fifteen cents each.

The clerk brought the box of fifty and I handed him a ten-dollar bill. He frowned and said, "That will be fifty dollars, sir." I grabbed my ten-dollar bill and beat a hasty retreat.

That night at dinner I told Hoke of my experience, and he and his wife got a big kick out of my tale. Then he told me, "Bill, I'm president of the Hava-Tampa Cigar Company and we make all of the Tampa cigars. The Tampa Diplomat is a special brand for U.S. politicians and foreign diplomats. The customer's name is imprinted on the wrapper instead of the words Tampa Diplomat." Hoke said he hadn't smoked in twenty years but he always carried Tampa Diplomats to give to his friends. As a footnote, all the time I was overseas, Hoke sent me a box of Tampa Diplomats every month. I shared them with Paul because we were the only two on the crew who smoked cigars.

Five years later, while I was stationed in Denver, Colorado, Hoke invited me to dinner at the Wilhurst Saddle Club, the home of the Hope Diamond. When I picked him up that night at his hotel, he told me that his dear wife of forty-six years had died the previous year. The next year I heard from a mutual friend that Hoke had died in a night club on Christmas Eve, surrounded by family and friends.

By the third day of our recruiting, we had our crew picked. Paul took their names to the director of operations, and he agreed to assign us as a combat crew. We were all eventually transferred across town to Drew Field, where we were issued an old B-17 and immediately began our combat crew flight training.

Our training went very smoothly. By the end of the month, it was apparent that Paul and I had done a good job of selecting a crew: We were named the "Outstanding Crew of the Month." As our reward, we were permitted to fly our B-17 to any location in the United States for the weekend. Our engineer, Amos, told us that his father lived in Houston, Texas, and was very ill. He said that he would really appreciate it if we would go there. We all agreed, knowing that Amos needed some time with his father before we went overseas.

Landing in Houston, we parked the aircraft in a secured area. We found that Amos' brother, Jake, had borrowed a small school bus to take all of us out to their ranch, south of Houston. After checking in with Base Operations, we all climbed into the bus for the ride to a real Texas ranch. Jake told us, "When the wind is from the right direction, the aircraft from the base fly right over the ranch, and usually at a very low altitude."

When we arrived at the ranch, Amos' mother and father greeted us like family and made us feel welcome. I had always heard about the friendliness of Texas people. We were to see it clearly demonstrated during our visit. After a wonderful dinner, most of us hit the sack because we were going hunting for jack rabbits the next morning.

We had all agreed to hunt in pairs at one-hour intervals or until one of the team members got a rabbit. Amos took Paul and me on the first run out across the prairie. We were each armed with a .22-caliber rifle with long rifle ammunition. Our hunting positions were rather precarious, as we were each draped over one of the front fenders of an old Model A Ford. Amos drove like he was on a speedway instead of in a pasture full of prairie dog holes and sagebrush.

Within the first half-hour of our wild ride, a huge jack rabbit jumped up on Paul's side and really took off on a zigzag course. Paul got off one shot, hit that jack rabbit in the back of the head, and sent it rolling for about twenty feet. I jumped off the fender and ran over to pick up the biggest rabbit I had ever seen. I am only 5'7, but when I grabbed the ears of that rabbit and draped it over my shoulder, the toes of its hind feet were on the ground. Amos had talked about hunting jack rabbits and how big they were, but we always thought it was just a big Texan telling Texas tales. Now I would have no problem in believing Amos' stories. Since Paul got the first jack rabbit on our team, we went back to the house so the other teams would have a chance to get one of those monsters.

After another team went out, a neighbor came over to see Amos and his combat crew. He introduced himself, saying, "Just call me Wyatt." He was probably in his mid or late sixties. I was admiring what he had driven up in – a black Model T Ford in mint condition – when Wyatt said, "If you think this is something, young fellow, come on back to the ranch with me and I'll show you something you won't believe."

I went back with him to his ranch and he took me out to the barn. When he opened the door, I was looking at a brand new Model T Ford sitting on blocks. It still wore the protective coating that was put on at the factory. Wyatt told me he bought the first three Model T Fords the Ford dealer in Houston received from the factory. He started using one and stored the other two in his barn. When the first one wore out, after more than 100,000 miles, he stripped it for parts and started using number-two. He said, "There's only 65,000 miles on number-two, so there's no telling when I'll have to start using number-three." He said the Model T's were the only cars he had ever owned. I didn't know if I was hearing another tall Texas tale. But, from what I saw, I had no reason to doubt this kind gentleman.

When we returned, Amos had just come in with the last team. No one else had come back with a jack rabbit. There was a lot of talk about the ones that got away, but Paul was the only one on the crew who had shot a Texas jack rabbit. There is a tourist joke in Texas about a jack-a-lope – a large, mounted jack rabbit head with antelope antlers. It makes a fun conversation piece, as long as you realize it is just another tall Texas tale. Our jack rabbit experience was no tall tale.

The weekend visit to a Texas ranch was over much too soon. Goodbyes and thank-yous were expressed with considerable emotion to some wonderful new friends. The flight back to Drew Field was almost uneventful. Mac, our navigator, allowed me to try my hand at low-altitude pilotage on the way home. I got us back to Tampa with no problems, but I had us lined up for an entry into an approach pattern for McDill Field instead of Drew Field. Luckily, Paul recognized the area and moved over to the approach pattern for Drew Field.

After we landed, we had a very pleasant surprise awaiting our return. The parents of one of our waist gunners, Bud Jones, had arrived for a visit and invited the entire crew to dinner at the Floridian Hotel. Since we were all pretty beat after our flight from Houston, we decided to make it the next evening.

The next night we had a great dinner with some wonderful people from Brooklyn, New York. Paul knew, but did not say anything to anyone until we were ready to leave the hotel, that our orders were in and we were scheduled to depart sometime the next day. That was a shock to all of us, even though we knew it could be anytime. We all thanked Mr. and Mrs. Jones for a most enjoyable evening and headed for the base. Bud stayed with his parents and caught a cab to the base a few hours later.

I was so cranked up with the excitement of what the next day would bring that I could hardly sleep that night.

Dinner with the Joneses

Crew of the Month

Top row (from left): Cpl. Amos Moore, chief engineer; Cpl. Bud Jones, waist gunner; Cpl. Lee Senk, radio operaator; Cpl. Ruff Hanchett, ball turret gunner; S/Sgt. Bill Cramer, chief armour; Cpl. Thor Pearson, tail gunner. Bottom row: 1st Lt. Paul Quinn, pilot; 2nd Lt. Don Howard, co-pilot; unknown former bombardier; 2nd Lt. Charlie McFarlin, navigator.

CHAPTER 6

En Route to War

After breakfast, Paul called us all together and said, "We have our orders to go to Hunter Field in Savannah, Georgia, to pick up a new B-17 to take to England." We were all excited to know that we would be flying overseas instead of going by boat like a herd of cattle. It allowed us the prestige of proving our airmanship by flying our own airplane that great distance. As the first crew to get their orders, we were being flown to Hunter instead of going by troop train.

Shortly after Paul's announcement, we were all sent to the supply room to be issued brand new flying equipment – everything, including a parachute and parachute bag, winter and summer flying suits, sunglasses, winter and summer helmets with goggles, a B-4 bag, two types of leather gloves with silk inserts, and best of all, a new leather A-2 jacket. We had all worn old flying suits and old A-2 jackets while in training.

We found out later, when the commanding officer came down to the flight line to see us off, that all of our special treatment was because we had been selected as the Outstanding Crew of the Month. That really gave us all a boost. Paul was so proud of the crew that he seemed to walk a foot off the ground.

The flight to Hunter was uneventful, although it certainly seemed odd for all of us to be flying in the back of a C-47. As we taxied up to the terminal, we passed seven beautiful silver B-17s parked in the revetment area. We all made bets on which one we would take to England and wrote down the tail number for the one each of us chose. None of us won because we found out that the one assigned to us was up in the air on a final test flight before our flight to England.

Since we arrived after 1800 hours, we all received our room assignments and then met in the air crew mess hall for dinner. Several of the guys went into town after dinner, but most of us decided to hit the sack because we were to start signing for our equipment at 0700 the next morning. Paul and I sat around talking over coffee for an hour after everyone else left. He said that he had found out from the duty officer that the processing wouldn't take long and we should be on our way before lunch. I think Paul was a little concerned about having to sign for a half-million dollar airplane. That was the first really serious talk between Paul and me since we had formed our own crew at Plant Park. I almost told him that night that I was a trained bombardier, but decided to never admit that fact to him.

I recalled that while I was at Tyndall Field, I had an opportunity to look at my service record and saw a notation pertaining to my bitterness about not being commissioned and about my throwing away the bombardier wings I had been issued. I always had a suspicion that Paul had checked the service records of the whole crew and that he knew I graduated from the Cadet Program as a bombardier. If Paul did know, he was probably waiting for me to get over my anger and tell him. After all, he did assign me to a nose position even though we had a bombardier assigned to the crew. That bombardier only lasted through the first three weeks of combat crew training. Paul kicked him off the crew because he was always drunk. He was good at bombing and finished all of the practice bombing missions before leaving our crew. I always suspected the guy was afraid of flying and just too proud to admit it, so he stayed drunk.

Since we were finished with the bombing portion of our combat crew training, Paul never asked for a replacement and I continued to ride the bombardier's seat during the remainder of our training. I am probably the only combat crew member who had his name on the back of his seat because the majority of the bombardier seats were made by the Cramer Furniture Manufacturing Company in Chicago. They weren't family, but it made a good conversation piece.

I don't think any of us needed a wake-up call because we were all excited about getting into our beautiful new B-17. After a quick breakfast, we headed for Base Operations and found that our B-17 had a Norden bombsight in the nose. Paul signed for the airplane and had me sign for the bombsight.

After piling our things into the bomb bay of that "big ass bird," we climbed aboard. Mac and I swung ourselves up into the nose via the front escape hatch and took up our positions. Mac was still flight planning for the first leg of our trip that would take us to Bangor, Maine, and the second leg that would take us to Goose Bay, Labrador. If the good weather held, we would be able to overfly Bangor and go directly to Goose Bay. Mac and I had decided to learn each other's jobs in case anything happened to one of us on a combat mission. I made it a point to observe him closely but stayed back so I would not get in his way.

Paul started the engines and we taxied out to the runway. It seemed that we had just turned on to the runway and locked the tail wheel when the control tower gave us takeoff instructions and wished us luck. As we climbed gracefully into the sky, Mac gave Paul the heading for Bangor and we all relaxed a little. The leg to Bangor was smooth and without a problem, but Paul decided to land at Bangor and take on additional fuel. Lee had picked up a message on his radio that bad weather was expected between Bangor and Goose Bay.

At Bangor, we had time to run into the flight line snack bar for a hamburger and milkshake. Amos had to stay with the aircraft during the refueling, so after I finished my snack I took him a hamburger and sat around on the ground with him while our beautiful bird was being refueled. An hour and a half after we landed, we were all back on board and ready for the next leg of our adventure.

Making a smooth takeoff, we climbed steadily to our cruising altitude. Mac already had the leg planned and gave Paul the heading for Goose Bay. He then showed me several navigation techniques and defined several principles of navigation. He told me that, at the first opportunity, he would teach me to use the sextant to "shoot the stars."

After talking navigation for quite a while, Mac suddenly said, "When are you going to teach me about the bombsight?"

"How about now?" I replied. I called Paul on the intercom and told him that I was turning on the bombsight so that Mac and I could play with it for a while. All he said was, "Roger."

I took the cover off the bombsight and turned on the power and had Mac look into the eyepiece. I explained that the cross hairs are called indices and showed him how to keep them apart with the two knurled knobs on the right side. I advised him, "Once the pilot turns on the PPI [planned position indicator] we must be sure the bombsight, the bomb panel and the bomb bay doors are coordinated. When the indices are permitted to meet, the bombs will drop automatically."

Mac asked, "Why is it that someone carrying around a bombsight is always seen wearing a side arm and usually being followed by a guy with a Thompson submachine gun?"

"It's my understanding," I replied, "that the tight security for the bombsight is merely to keep it from falling into enemy hands because the real secret of the Norden bombsight is in the ratio of the gears." I then pointed out the red destruct button on the bombsight and told him, "Due to the ratio of the gears being classified, the bombsight contains an explosive charge. If the aircraft has to land in unfriendly territory, the bombardier must push the red destruct button to destroy the gears. After pushing the button, there is only three minutes to get out of and away from the ship before the bombsight and probably the whole nose of the aircraft are destroyed."

We were getting close to Goose Bay when we ran into some really rough weather. I turned off the bombsight, replaced the cover, and strapped myself on my seat. Paul called everyone on the intercom and told us to stay in our positions and to put on our seat belts. After about an hour and a half of bouncing around the sky, we broke into the clear just before entering the landing pattern at Goose Bay. Our landing was very gentle. Paul really knew how to grease a B-17 onto a runway.

Paul decided we would draw straws to see who would remain in the ship all night because of the bombsight being on board. No one was looking forward to a night in an icy aircraft, so I told Paul, "I know how to remove and install the bombsight and I can babysit it in my room for the night."

Everyone was relieved and Paul laughingly said, "Why do you think I had him sign for the damn thing?"

After dinner we all hit the showers and then turned in for the night. Even though I had to go to bed wearing my side arm, and sleep with the bombsight under my bed all night, it sure was better than one of us sleeping in a cold aircraft.

Early the next morning, after I reinstalled the bombsight, we took off for our next destination: Reykjavik, Iceland. Again, we hit very bad weather and were quite relieved when we landed safely. I didn't have to sleep with the bombsight that night because the base commander had a walk-in safe and allowed us to store it in the safe overnight.

That night, after dinner, the crew decided to go to a movie on base. At Reykjavik, the only place to see one was on base. On the way to the theater, the driver found out that we had just arrived, so he took us to the Officers' Club to show us the only tree in Iceland. There it stood, in all its regal splendor, made out of two-by-fours and paper.

When we got to the theater, I started reading the show bill about the movie, the name of which I do not recall. There, before my eyes, was a picture and the name of an old girlfriend from Cincinnati, Georgia Lee Settle. I pointed out the show bill to the rest of the crew and told them, "She was my first girlfriend when we were both in the fifth grade. Georgia Lee and I drifted apart and dated other people after we entered Withrow High School. I heard some years later that she had won a screen test after graduating from Withrow and was making movies in Hollywood."

After the movie, in which Georgia Lee had only a supporting role, the crew agreed she was good and would probably go far in Hollywood. We then took a vote and decided to name our airplane *Georgia Lee.* After leaving the movie, we hit the sack due to an early morning takeoff time.

I proceeded to the base commander's office after breakfast, retrieved the bombsight from the duty officer, and installed it in the nose of our aircraft. The rest of the crew arrived a short time later, and we took off in our big bird for the next leg. Once we were airborne, we began to circle the field and Paul told everyone we would have to go back due to a mechanical problem that shouldn't take long to fix. On the final approach the tower called us on the radio and told us our tail wheel was not down. However, they cleared us to land and advised Paul to hold the tail off the ground as long as possible and then let it down gently. Never having been in a no-tail-wheel landing before, we all put on our seat belts and sweated. Our touchdown was purposely a little harder than usual to try to make the tail wheel drop down. We bounced off the runway and then hit again. That time, Paul pushed forward on the yoke to keep the aircraft from bouncing up in the air again, because we were just about out of runway. As the aircraft slowed down, the tail dropped and made contact with the runway, causing an awful crackling metal sound. As soon as the ship stopped, we all jumped out and looked at it. There was a big bend in the middle. Our beautiful new B-17 looked like a banana.

Since we were a combat crew, there was an immediate FEB (Flying Evaluation Board) to determine if the accident was caused by pilot error, in which case he would be charged for the cost of repairing the aircraft. The whole crew waited in the outer room while Paul testified and the FEB deliberated. They decided there was no cause for a finding of pilot error, so Paul was off the hook. We learned that the base commander was a real B-17 nut and had been looking for a way to get one for his base. He decided to have it repaired and to keep it on his base. He signed for the bombsight as well.

The next day we climbed aboard a C-54 for our trip to Scotland and then England. What an emotional letdown; we were just sick about not being able to fly overseas in our own aircraft. But when we arrived at Polebrook Air Base, Station 110, we found that none of the crews who brought their own aircraft over got to take them into combat. New crews flew old aircraft. That's just the way it was.

We were assigned crew quarters and were told that we would have a full day of indoctrination starting the next day. Practice missions would fill the next several days, and our first combat mission could be as early as the first of the next week.

During our training before starting combat flying, we found a good artist in another squadron and he painted "nose art" on the back of our A-2 jackets. There she sat, Georgia Lee, riding on top of a big B-17. I sent the real Georgia Lee a photo of the back of my A-2 jacket and a letter explaining why we named our first airplane after her. She wrote back about how thrilled she was, having a B-17 named after her. She brought me up to date on her life in Hollywood, her three divorces, and her parents. She asked me to stop and see her at the RKO Studios if I got out her way. She didn't say a thing about the fact that the Georgia Lee riding on top of the B-17 was completely nude.

Original A-2 jacket – fifty years later.

CHAPTER 7

The Beginning of Air Combat

Our first morning of indoctrination covered many subjects: getting along with our English hosts, history of the 351st Bomb Group, the number of missions flown, targets hit, and, of course, VD lectures. After the VD lectures, I felt it might be advisable to put on a pair of rubber gloves before shaking hands with any of the girls I should chance to meet.

Walking around the base in the afternoon, I had a very pleasant surprise when I ran into the newly promoted Capt. Clark Gable. He invited me to the Church Army Canteen (the English equivalent of our Salvation Army back home) for tea and rolls.

The first thing he said when we sat down was, "I like your mustache, are you trying to copy mine?"

"Yes," I said, "but I have to darken mine with burnt cork."

Captain Gable told me that he and Andy were sent to Fort Wright in Spokane for photography training after leaving Tyndall Field. From there, to Pueblo, Colorado, to join the 351st Bomb Group. They later shipped to England with a cadre of 351st personnel. He said, "We have been making a movie of the 351st Bomb Group in combat and I have flown four combat missions, so far." He told me that Andy still loved flying and that they had one more combat mission to fly in the next few days before going back to the States to put the movie in the can. "The name of the movie will be *Combat America,*" he said, "and you should be sure to see it when you return to the States – especially since you are now part of the 351st Bomb Group." I learned that Captain Gable, like me, enlisted in the Army Air Corps as a private. That was several months after his wife, Carole Lombard, was killed in an airplane crash while on a War Bond tour. He said, "I later went to OCS, where I received my commission, then to Gunnery School, where you and I first met."

After two cups of tea and four rolls with marmalade, it was time for me to leave for my training mission. Captain Gable and I shook hands and wished each other luck. He said, "Bill, you be sure to come see me at MGM if you ever get to Hollywood." It is one of my biggest regrets that I never had the opportunity to see him again, except in the movies.

Our second and third days of training were spent in an old B-17E. She must have been one of the originals in the group, but she flew very smoothly. Takeoffs and landings, takeoffs and landings, and then more of the same. Our fourth day was formation flying in the same B-17E. We must have been pretty good, because we only had one day of practice at formation flying. Of course, the whole crew knew that Paul was one hell of a pilot and that there was nowhere we would not go with him.

Our first combat mission was to Wilhelmshaven. The feeling was one of exhilaration for me, because that was the day I had been training for since I had enlisted: combat with the enemy. Our group lost only one aircraft to enemy fighters and none to flak.

Even though our assigned aircraft had a bombsight, I had been told to salvo my bombs when the lead bombardier dropped his bombs. That day, as was my habit, when I dropped the bombs, I watched the lights on the bomb panel go out one by one. When the last one went out, I pushed the salvo switch as a means of clearing out any of the bombs that may have hung in the bomb racks. I then called Lee in the radio room and asked him to check the bomb bay to be sure all the bombs were gone before I closed the bomb bay doors. Lee called me back with, "The bomb racks are clear." I responded with, "Roger," and closed the bomb bay doors. We then headed for home. Paul made a textbook, three-point landing on the first part of the runway.

After parking in our assigned spot, we went to the interrogation room. Everyone there was talking about Captain Gable being on the mission with us that day. So I got to fly one combat mission with him. That was his last mission; he had already departed for London, en route to Hollywood, with the combat footage he had shot. It was regrettable that there had been no opportunity for me to introduce him to my crew.

We all received our combat ration (a shot of whiskey) and headed for a sit-down meeting with one of the people from the Intelligence Office. There was not much for us to report because our part of the formation was not hit by German fighters and we saw very little flak in our part of the sky. After the debriefing, we all went back to our aircraft to unload and clean our guns. No mission was ever over until we cleaned our guns so they would be ready for the next mission.

Four days after our first mission, the second was to bomb the marshaling yards at Wesel. The veteran combat crews would call that a "milk run," as we encountered no German fighters and the flak was very meager and inaccurate. All the aircraft returned with no injured on board.

As I was cleaning my nose gun after a very short period of interrogation, I suddenly developed a severe pain in my cheekbone below my right eye. Amos gave me a couple of APCs (an Army pill that was a little stronger than aspirin), and by the time we finished with our guns, the pain had subsided.

Our third mission was to Bremen, referred to as "Little B" as a comparison with "Big B," which was Berlin. Both were very rough targets. Just prior to the target we were jumped by Me 109s and FW 190s. We all had our first opportunity to shoot at enemy fighters but none were shot down. After the German fighters left, the flak became very intense; several aircraft were hit and one went down in the target area. We got back without damage or injury to any of our crew.

Three combat missions and I had not yet experienced fear. I wondered why. Perhaps it was because I was always so busy with the bombs and nose gun during the time I should have been aware of fear.

While cleaning my guns after interrogation, I again felt the sharp pain in my cheekbone. I began to think that the solvent we used to clean the guns might be the cause of my problem. I decided not to eat dinner that night because the pain was so intense. I took a couple of APCs and went to bed.

Mission number-four was to Emden. Thirty-four B-17s hit the target with excellent results. A few German fighters were seen in the distance and the flak was moderate but inaccurate. All of our aircraft returned safely and with no casualties. After going to interrogation and taking care of our guns, some of us headed to the mess hall for dinner. We were sitting around having coffee when the pain in my right cheekbone hit again. The mess sergeant, who was at the table with us, gave me a couple of APCs and told me to take them with my coffee. Since we had another mission in the morning, I decided to go to bed and try to get rid of the pain.

Our fifth mission was a tough one. We were sent to Ludwigshafen to bomb the IG Farbenin chemical plant and I knew that we would be in the air for eight hours or more. On that mission our group put thirty-six planes in the air. Flak in the target area was intense and fairly accurate, causing us to lose two aircraft.

After we left enemy territory and dropped down below 10,000 feet, I took off my oxygen mask and the pain in my right cheekbone really hit me. Mac saw me with my head in my hands and asked, "What's wrong, Bill? Did you get hit? Are you OK?"

"I've been having this lousy pain in my cheekbone for about a week and it seems to be getting worse each time it hits me," I said.

He opened the first-aid kit we kept in the nose and gave me two APCs. He then called Paul to tell him about my problem. Paul said to me, "After interrogation you are to go to the hospital to see what is causing the problem and I will take care of the nose gun for you."

We landed at the base without incident and, after a long interrogation, I headed for the hospital. They ran some tests, took some x-rays, and told me I would have to stay overnight for more tests. After dinner, Paul and a couple of the other fellows came over to see me but when they saw how much pain I was in they cut their visit short.

The next morning, I got the bad news. The doctor said, "You have an acute infection and blockage in your frontal sinus. Since there is no natural drainage in that area, the only treatment is an operation to make a 'window' in your right frontal sinus."

Paul came over after breakfast and told me he was heading for London, as our crew was not scheduled to fly another mission for at least three days. I told him what the doctor had said and that I would be transferred to the 303rd General Hospital later that day. We talked for a long time about getting him a new bombardier and who I would probably be flying with when I got out of the hospital. Paul must have said something to the rest of the crew because they all came over to wish me well on my trip to the general hospital.

On the bomb run.

CHAPTER 8

A Pause in My War

The 303rd General Hospital was a big facility set in a very picturesque English countryside. It had the latest equipment and was staffed with a great crew of doctors and nurses. I was checked in and assigned to a ward where they ran more tests and took more x-rays.

My period in the hospital gave me time to reflect on what I had accomplished since I started flying combat. Not much. Five combat missions and we had dropped twelve 500-pound bombs on each of the missions. I had dropped fifteen tons of high explosives on Germany and they were still kicking our butts. We had put up thirty-six aircraft and only twenty-eight returned. Other bomb groups suffered much worse losses; the 100th Bomb Group suffered 100 percent losses for a period of time. We were told the 351st Bomb Group's losses were "acceptable." I would have liked for someone to define an "acceptable loss" to me. If we lost eight aircraft on a combat mission, the aircraft could be replaced. But how could we replace those eighty young Americans?

"I'll be operating on you in the morning and you will get relief from all that pain you have been having," the doctor broke my chain of thought and I was glad he did. "I know what you have been going through because another doctor performed the same operation on me in this very hospital last year." I was glad to hear that. The pain in my cheekbone had been severe and continuous since I turned into the hospital at the base.

That night the nurse gave me a sleeping pill, the first and last one I've ever taken. The same nurse awakened me in the morning and I was allowed to shave and shower but not eat.

After I got back in bed, she gave me a shot of morphine. A few minutes later I couldn't care less what they wanted to do to me. I remember being wheeled on the dolly and parked along a wall. After I was moved into the operating room and placed on the operating table, a board was attached to the table. My arm was strapped to the board and a needle was inserted to inject something into my vein. I found out later that they also gave me ether prior to the operation.

When I regained my senses, I found it was the day after the operation. My old pain was now replaced by a new pain—the pain of having a hole drilled into my skull through a nostril. I was not permitted out of bed for five days and I was to remain in the hospital for one month, barring complications. After the first week there I was about to go mad until I found some fellow patients with whom I could play gin rummy, hearts, and bridge. That helped to pass the time.

My crew came to see me during my third week there and they brought my A-2 jacket, in case I wanted to take some walks in the countryside. They told me they picked up a newly arrived bombardier three days after I left for the hospital and they now had fifteen missions under their belt.

Before leaving, Paul told me, "We have all checked out as a lead crew and we're now really getting in the missions." He told me to hurry up and get out of the hospital so that I could at least fly the last missions with them. I asked him about his new bombardier and all he would say was, "He's just temporary until you get out of the hospital." Paul also told me, "Bill, we did a real good job in selecting our combat crew." Those two remarks really gave me a good feeling.

In the morning I awoke with the pleasant thought that I only had another week in this hospital. I was now able to walk around the hospital, inside and outside. I had just gotten the news that there was to be an outside concert with Maj. Glenn Miller and his band that afternoon, so I made plans to attend with some of my card-playing buddies.

The band was excellent. All those songs reminded us of home and our school dances. Later in the afternoon, the commanding officer of the hospital came to the ward. He told me, "Your squadron sent this Air Medal for me to present to you for flying your first five combat missions."

One day before being discharged from the hospital, I woke up in a happy mood and had breakfast. More tests were run, after which the doctor told me, "I have bad news for you. You've got a case of the mumps."

Incredulously I asked, "Isn't that a childhood disease, Doc?"

"Yes, but it isn't limited to children," he said. "You'll meet some patients in the ward who are in their thirties and forties." He then told me to count on at least three more weeks in the hospital for me to get rid of the mumps.

A transfer to the contagious ward made me feel like a helpless kid. I don't know when I had been more miserable. That afternoon, the nurse telephoned my crew at the base to let them know what had happened.

Air Medal

During my second week of isolation, my crew came to see me. We had to speak through a big glass panel with a sterile screen between us. They told me that they had finished their combat missions without any casualties and they were heading home the next day. I was very happy for them but very sad to know they would not be around when I got out of that damn hospital. Before leaving, Paul gave the nurse a slip of paper for me that had a name on it and he told me through the screen, "The guy is a damn good pilot and he's looking for a bombardier." He winked at me as they all turned to leave. We didn't even have a chance to shake hands for the last time.

Another ten days passed before I was released from the hospital. After I was back at the base for a couple of hours, the squadron clerk came to my barracks to tell me that the commanding officer, Major Ledoux, wanted to see me at his office.

When I reported to Major Ledoux, he told me, "The flight surgeon does not want you to do any high-altitude flying for a while—at least until he is sure the window in your nose has properly healed." The terrible sinking feeling I had must have been apparent in my face. Major Ledoux then asked me, "Do you think you could handle a rough, five-week, very intensified radar and navigation course at an RAF school down near Dover?" I jumped at the chance because it would probably be that long before the flight surgeon let me go back to flying. I thanked Major Ledoux enthusiastically for considering me for the course.

The Radar/Navigation School at RAF Hawkinge was a very rapid-fire, no-nonsense course taught by RAF personnel who were all combat veterans. I was one of only three Americans, or Yanks, as our hosts called us, who were in the class. I felt a little out of place because the other two Americans were majors and the British and Canadian students were also officers with the exception of two RAF flying sergeants.

Our first three weeks were devoted to navigation, ten to twelve hours per day plus some nights for celestial navigation. Our last two weeks dealt with radar, "black box," "G box," and "Mickey." I had no idea why those names were chosen, but those were all techniques for bombing and navigation through the use of radar.

Our graduation was very formal and was followed by a reception. Afterwards, I headed back to Polebrook, looking forward to getting back on a combat crew and back up in the air. Finishing what I started out to do – to complete a combat tour in a B-17 – was very important to me. Now it was going to take me a little longer because, while I was in the hospital, the combat tour was raised from thirty to thirty-five missions.

After returning to Polebrook, and going to my squadron's Orderly Room, I was informed by the clerk that Major Ledoux wanted to see me the minute I arrived from RAF Hawkinge. He also told me, in a very confidential tone, "You're sure in hot water for keeping the old man in the dark about your being trained as a bombardier."

When I reported to Major Ledoux, it was with a great deal of trepidation. He walked around his desk and ripped the T/Sgt. stripes off both of my sleeves. I knew I was in trouble, but I didn't expect it to be *this* serious. The major then told me to sit down as he took a seat on the edge of his desk.

The first thing he wanted to know was, "Why didn't you tell your pilot that you graduated from the Cadet Program as a bombardier?"

"Major Ledoux," I answered, "I guess the reason was because I felt betrayed by the Army since I was not commissioned like my classmates when I graduated." I added, "If the Army had been honest with me and advised me in the beginning that I was too young to receive a commission, I probably would have gone through the program anyway because all I have ever wanted to do is fly."

Major Ledoux told me that he and my former pilot, Paul Quinn, were good friends. Before Paul left for the States, the two of them had a long talk about how to handle my situation.

At that point, I really expected a court-martial. Instead, Major Ledoux could not hold in his little joke any longer. He chuckled to himself, reached into his desk drawer, and came over to me with a card containing two U.S. and two Wing and Prop lapel insignia. He handed me the card and then pinned second lieutenant bars on my shoulders. He told me, "Paul convinced me to initiate the paperwork to get you a battlefield commission and to restore you to bombardier status. This was all started even before you went to RAF Hawkinge. Everything was approved last week except the commission. An age waiver had to be obtained from the War Department since you still are not twenty-one years of age. The waiver was approved and the commission arrived this morning." He then asked me, "Will you be willing to fly with new crews as a bombardier, radar operator or navigator for a while

Before receiving battlefield commission.

HEADQUARTERS
U. S. FORCES, EUROPEAN THEATER

AG 201 — CRAMER, WILLIAM L. (O) 10 April 1944

SUBJECT: Appointment in the Army of the United States

To: 2nd Lt William L. Cramer, Jr. 0-2033061
Seckenheim School Center, APO 403, US Army

1. The Secretary of War has directed that you be informed that the President has appointed and commissioned you a temporary Second Lieutenant in the Army of the United States effective 10 April 1944. This appointment may be vacated at any time by the President and, unless sooner terminated, is for the duration of the present emergency and six months thereafter. Your serial number is 0-2033061, and you will rank from 10 April 1944.

2. This letter should be retained by you as evidence of your appointment as no commissions will be issued during the emergency.

BY COMMAND OF GENERAL MCNARNEY:

George F. Herbert
GEORGE F. HERBERT
Colonel, AGD
Adjutant General

e: This is a Battle Field Commission.
Officer is promoted from the grade of T/Sgt.

and help us determine why there is such a shortage of people who can put the bombs on the target?"

With a sigh of relief I said, "Major Ledoux, I'll fly with anyone you want me to fly with and in any position as long as I get to fly combat and not just instruct."

He advised me that I would be assigned to a regular crew as soon as we got the people hitting the targets. The major then said, "Meet me at the Officers' Club tonight, Bill, and it will be my pleasure to buy you dinner to help celebrate your new gold bars."

I accepted with gratitude. I tried to express my appreciation to Major Ledoux for his confidence in me, but he cut me off.

"Bill, we are just trying to rectify a wrong," he said, as I was leaving his office. Then he added, "Of course, you'll be expected to buy drinks for everyone at the bar."

While Major Ledoux and I were having dinner, several people came over to our table. He introduced me to them and briefly told them the story of my new bars. While we were having our after-dinner coffee, Major Ledoux handed me a card with three pair of wings on it—one was bombardier, one was navigator, and one had a circle in the center.

"The one with a circle is called Observer wings and they are now being worn by the radar people," he said. "You are probably the only second lieutenant in the Army who is authorized to wear all three."

I reminded him, "Plus my gunner wings."

"Yes, plus your gunner wings," he answered. "My God, a second lieutenant authorized four different pair of wings . . . What's this Army coming to?"

Before we went into the bar, the squadron operations officer came by the table. Major Ledoux introduced us and told him, "Here's a new trouble-shooter for you. He will help us find out why we are not getting our bombs on the target. Start him flying with some new crews as soon as you can get him on the combat crew schedule."

When we entered the bar, it was packed. It seemed as though the word got around very quickly when free drinks were available. That was a day and a night I will remember for a long time.

CHAPTER 9

Rejoining the Fight

The operations officer did not take long in getting me back up in the air. My sixth mission was my first mission as a new second lieutenant, and I was assigned to a new crew from the States. We went to Schweinfurt in the *Buckeye Babe,* a beautifully maintained B-17F, and on her ninety-ninth combat mission. She later went down in the North Sea on her 103rd mission. In later years, at a 351st Bomb Group reunion in St. Louis, I met Hershel Dunmire, the crew chief of the *Buckeye Babe.* Hershel was very proud of the fact that the *Babe* never had to abort a mission due to mechanical problems. I have never known any other crew chief that could make that kind of statement.

Our group put up sixteen planes that day and we were assigned to fly in the low box, which is where new crews usually fly. The crew's own bombardier was grounded due to a sinus problem, and I flew in his position. It sure was a boost to my morale to be able to handle a bombsight again. We learned later that the bombing results were good.

Suddenly, we were jumped by about sixty to seventy German fighters, Me 109s and FW 190s. They attacked mostly from our front, in what was described as a "company front" attack. They fired machine guns, 20mm cannons, and rockets at us, causing considerable damage to the formation. Four Me 109s made a company front attack on our ship, using headlight tracers. Since that was the first time I had ever seen machine-gun bullets coming at me, it shook me up so much that I froze on the trigger while firing at the four attacking enemy fighters. One of them blew up right in front of us, and I was given credit for shooting down a German fighter. The crew thought that was the greatest thing since ice cream—their bombardier shooting down an enemy fighter. I never did tell them, or anyone else, that I just froze on the trigger because I had never seen headlight tracers before or German bastards shooting at me.

The flak over the target was moderately effective, and several ships in the formation were hit. Our ship received several flak holes in the tail section, but the tail gunner was not injured. It just scared the hell out of him.

After leaving the target area, the trip back home was uneventful, with only slight damage from flak over the target and no injuries. The pilot made a smooth landing at Polebrook. When we entered the interrogation hut, the gunners were all running around telling everyone that their bombardier had shot down a German fighter with a single nose gun.

My seventh mission was to Berlin—the Big B. The group again put up sixteen planes. Colonel Romig led the group and we flew as the number-three ship in the lead box on this eight and one-half hour mission. My crew that day needed only one more mission to finish their combat tour of thirty-five missions. It was a relief to be flying with an experienced crew. We were all elated to know that we were taking our bomb load to the heart of Nazi Germany.

On that mission, I was assigned as the radar operator and my job was to jam the German radar to keep them from vectoring their fighters into our formation. En route to the target we did not see any German fighters, and the flak was meager and ineffective. Over the target was a different story. We had intense and accurate flak, and many ships in our formation received considerable damage. My radar jamming apparently had little or no effect on the German 88s that filled the sky with flak so thick that one could almost use it as a landing strip.

Just after the bombardier dropped his bombs and said, "Bombs away," we heard a loud explosion and the ship began to shudder. My radar station was in the waist of the aircraft, just aft of the radio room, so I was not able to see anything. The radio operator opened his door and told us we took a direct hit between the number-one and number-two engines. Both engines were on fire; however, the pilot was able to get the fires extinguished and the engines were still operating even though they sounded very rough.

Barely able to keep up with the rest of the formation, we had a long trip ahead of us. We had to be very careful with any maneuver. In trying to keep up with the others, we began throwing things overboard that were not essential. However, it was still too early to throw out our guns and ammunition. We had other damaged aircraft in the formation and were attempting to avoid known heavy flak areas such as Potsdam, Magdeburg, Hannover, and Dusseldorf. On our way out of Germany, over Munster, our ship received more flak damage and the pilots were having a hard time maintaining our altitude. Over Antwerp, we began throwing out all the guns and ammunition, except for the guns in the tail and nose. We made it to Calais before the pilot had to feather number-one and number-two engines. We were beginning to lose altitude more rapidly, so we threw out the nose and tail guns as we headed for the "White Cliffs of Dover."

While at RAF Hawkinge, we had been allowed some free time from our studies one Sunday and I had visited those White Cliffs. I called the pilot on the intercom to give him an idea how high and treacherous, due to down drafts, those cliffs were. He said he thought we could make it OK as long as we did not lose any more altitude. The bombardier, from his position in the nose, could see the cliffs as they loomed up in front of us, and he was keeping the crew informed on the intercom. We were so low at that point that I suggested to the pilot that we jettison all of our parachutes because they sure would be of no use to us at that low altitude. He agreed. No one knows if getting rid of the chutes was of any help, but we hoped every little bit might be worthwhile. Looking out the waist window as we crossed the tops of those cliffs, the ground was so close that everyone raised up a little on their seats and lifted their feet.

The pilot had to make a wheels-up landing in a plowed field on the top of the White Cliffs due to a severed hydraulic line that prevented lowering our landing gear. When the aircraft stopped bouncing over the dirt field, we all piled out in a hurry, with nothing more than a few bumps and bruises.

The British Coastal Watch people at that location had already notified our base and were sending a C-47 to pick us up at an RAF base just north of Dover. They also arranged for a school bus to take us on a thirty-five-mile ride to the RAF base.

While we were standing around waiting, I asked an elderly gentleman how they knew what base to call. He just pointed his pipe stem at the tail of our ship and the big triangle J painted there. It seemed the Coastal Watch people knew the bomb groups and bases from the tail markings. There will always be a special place in my heart for the British people and especially the kind folks at that Coastal Watch station. They did their best to make us as comfortable as possible with conversation, tea, and crumpets while we awaited the bus to take us to the RAF base.

One might have expected a day of rest after a crash landing, but no such luck. The next day, on mission number-eight, I had another radar flight, this time to Kassel. The crew I was to fly with that day was another replacement crew from the States flying their first combat mission. To them I must have seemed to be a real veteran, with seven missions under my belt, and they asked me loads of questions. I tried to answer them without making my answers sound like war stories. All of the officers on this crew were second lieutenants, so I fit right in with them.

The whole crew had heard about my crash landing the day before and the pilot said, "Why in hell are you flying the day after a crash landing?"

My reply was, "Because we only have two trained Mickey [radar] operators in our entire bomb squadron and I am one of them."

After the briefing, we headed for the armament shop to pick up our guns. When we got to our ship, I had to help the ball turret gunner load his guns because he was so nervous his hands were shaking. He asked me not to say anything to the rest of the crew about his nervousness, and I assured him that he need not worry about that because I was just as nervous.

Our position in the formation was in the low box. The trip to and from the target was fairly routine, and we saw only three or four enemy fighters off in the distance. Over the target we encountered accurate flak, and five of our ships were damaged. Our return to Polebrook was uneventful. After our mission interrogation and gun cleaning, the crew invited me to go to town with them to celebrate their first combat mission.

The first thing every combat crew member did upon arriving at Polebrook air base was to get a bicycle, usually by buying it from someone going back to the States. We all got on our bicycles and I was appointed the leader, since none of them had yet been off base.

Our first and only stop was at my favorite pub, the Rose and Crown, in the town of Oundle. I introduced the crew to John, the owner, and we had many beers. John brought us all sandwiches of freshly baked bread with corned beef, cheese, sliced onion, and hot British mustard. He told his new customers, "This is your mate's favorite and maybe you chaps will enjoy it. The next time you stop by you may see 'Bill's Sandwich' on my menu."

The crew members, one and two at a time, met and left with local girls. The girl I had dated a couple of times was John's youngest daughter. However, she attended school in a nearby city and was only home on weekends. I was not scheduled to fly the next day, so I played darts with John and drank ale.

John taught me the fine art of drinking ale. The necessary items are a stein of ale, a roaring fire in the fireplace, and a poker. The poker is left in the fireplace until it is red hot. It is then inserted in the stein until it stops steaming. I never did learn if the heat of the poker caused a chemical change in the ale, but it was one fine drink.

After closing time, I stepped outside and noticed that the cold air did not have the usual sobering effect on me; in fact, just the opposite. Missing my bike the first time I reached for it told me I was in trouble, but I mounted it anyway and started pedaling for the base. I almost made it, but just prior to reaching the main gate, my bike decided to leave the road and we fell into a hedgerow. I decided it would be too difficult to get out of there in the dark, so I just slept there all night. My big, heavy GI overcoat and the alcohol in my system were probably the only things that kept me from freezing to death.

Early morning truck traffic on the road woke me the next day. I got out of the hedgerow, back on my bike, and headed for the base—with quite a hangover.

After a three-day stand-down, mission number-nine for me was to hit the railroad depot and marshaling yards at Hamm. It was to be a radar bombing mission, so it gave me a chance, as a bombardier, to use what I had learned about radar bombing at RAF Hawkinge. Although the crew and I had the same number of missions, it certainly had not taken them as long to get theirs completed. No enemy fighters were seen, and flak—even over the target—was inaccurate.

After landing, we had a short mission interrogation and I headed for the air crew mess hall for dinner and then to the Officers' Club. At the bar I saw a friend, Pete, who was the copilot on another crew. Pete suggested, "Let's challenge my pilot and navigator to a few hands of bridge." As usual, Pete and I beat them and we won a few dollars. After the card game, Pete said he wasn't scheduled to fly for several days. I then suggested that we go to London and spend some of our bridge winnings. It was agreed we would meet for breakfast and then head for London.

The base bus took us to Peterborough, where we caught a train (the *Royal Scot*) for London. We arrived in London late in the afternoon and I asked Pete, "How about getting a room at the Red Cross Club before we start hitting the pubs?" Because it was always very difficult to find your way around London at night in the blackout, Pete thought that was a good idea. We had no trouble getting rooms, and Pete told me, "I'm going to call a couple of girls I know at the American Embassy." The girls agreed to meet us at the Red Cross Club for dinner. Since a dance was scheduled there that night, we decided that was preferable to pub hopping.

I went to our room to get some rest while Pete roamed around the lobby area. Awaking late and suddenly, I jumped out of bed, splashed cold water in my face, put on my uniform, and headed for the dining room. Pete was already there with the girls from the Embassy. After making my apology to everyone for oversleeping, we had a very enjoyable dinner with pleasant company and then moved into the ballroom for dancing.

Sitting at a nearby table was Fred, the ball turret gunner on the crew I went to Schweinfurt with on my first mission as a new second lieutenant. He was sitting with a Canadian sergeant and two girls in RAF uniforms. I excused myself to go over to say hello to him. I didn't know it before, but Fred had a split thumb on his right hand which operated like two separate fingers. He could pick up things with his thumb. While I was standing at the table, Fred was going to pay the waitress and picked up a pound note with his split thumb. She took one look at it, let out a shriek, and would not go back to that table the rest of the evening. That night Fred had met Elbert, a Canadian gunnery sergeant from the RCAF who had a split left thumb that was just as dexterous as Fred's right one.

Before I left their table, Fred had to tell everyone within hearing distance that I shot down a German fighter during the mission we were on together. There was some applause and shouts of "Good show!" from several RAF guys that were near enough to hear Fred.

Pete also heard Fred's remarks. "You didn't tell me you shot down a German fighter," he said.

"What's there to tell? I'm a trained aerial gunner."

The rest of the evening, we could not buy a drink at our table. We never did see who was sending the drinks over, but any time we got up to dance we had fresh drinks at the table when we returned. We finally decided to just relax and enjoy the free drinks because we were not able to find out who to thank for their generosity.

Later in the evening, Fred and Elbert got on the crowded dance floor with their dates and they both used their split thumbs to pinch girls dancing nearby just to hear them scream. Probably the only other person in the club who realized what was going on was me. I began to laugh so hard at each screech, I had to tell Pete and the girls about the two split thumbs. They thought it was hilarious. Now every time a girl screamed on the dance floor, everyone at our table had a fit of laughter. That caused everyone around us to start laughing. We all agreed that we had never before been in a place with so much screaming and laughing at the same time.

The ballroom was about to close, so we called a cab and took the girls to the apartment they shared. When we returned to the Red Cross Club, Pete and I stopped in the restaurant for some tea and tarts before we hit the sack. Before we left, Fred and his friend from the RCAF joined us. They really were a couple of clowns. Fred started out showing us how he stirred his tea by holding the spoon in his thumb. Elbert had to top him by holding his knife in his thumb and cutting a piece of toast. Everyone in the restaurant gathered around the table to watch the dexterous thumb feats.

Pete and I slipped out and went to our room. We had flipped a coin earlier to see who would have to climb into the upper. I lost. It did not take either of us long to drop off to sleep, but about two hours later there was one hell of an explosion. The whole building shook, windows broke, and I was knocked out of the upper bunk onto the floor. My crash landing was on my rear end, and it really caused considerable pain for a couple of hours. It was a good thing I was sleeping when it happened; I probably would have broken an arm or a leg trying to break my fall if I had been awake.

Pete and I got dressed and went downstairs to see what had happened. We learned that one of the German V-1 rockets crashed into an apartment building just a block away. The rocket did a tremendous amount of damage and killed fifteen people who lived in the building. I decided I was ready to go back to flying combat.

Back in our room, a chamber maid had brought each of us four blankets because most of the windows had been broken out and it was even colder than my night in the hedgerow. At breakfast we talked about how the brave English people—men, women, and children—had been going through that kind of brutal destruction and death for the past three or four years. After breakfast we packed up, checked out, and headed for the train to take us back to the base.

Mission number-ten for me was to Rheims, France, on the day before my twentieth birthday. We put up eighteen aircraft that afternoon, and Major Fishburne led the low box in a composite wing formation. My crew was another new crew from the States with no combat missions to their credit. My job was to be the radar navigator and to observe and evaluate the bombardier during the bomb run. The mission was almost like a practice mission—no flak and no enemy fighters. A great mission for a new crew, one that might give them enough self-confidence for the rougher missions to follow. The bombardier did a fine job, even though he merely had to salvo his bombs when the lead bombardier dropped his, using a bombsight. The bombardier's actions reflected good training and he was very competent, as my report after landing would indicate.

After an uneventful flight home and a short interrogation session, hitting the sack seemed like a good idea. I had another mission the next day.

As it turned out, the next mission was scrubbed due to bad weather. After breakfast, the squadron clerk came to my room and told me, "Captain Robinson would like to see you if you have a few minutes."

Robbie was seated at his desk, drinking coffee, and had already poured one for me. He started our discussion with, "Tell me about the crews we have been getting from the States and that you have been flying with lately."

"If the ones I have been with are any kind of indication, it appears we are getting some fine, well-trained people for our squadron," I replied.

Robbie agreed and then asked, "How did you enjoy your first radar navigation mission yesterday?"

"Great. That was the first time I had a chance to really use my navigation training. But you should pay me double – navigation and instructor bombardier."

"Boy, you sure are greedy," he replied. "Look, Bill, I don't have you scheduled to fly again until 7 May, so why don't you take a trip to London and blow off some steam?" That sure sounded like a good idea to me. As I was leaving his office, Robbie shouted, "Happy birthday! Are you old enough to vote yet?"

I waved goodbye to him and said, "Next year."

A friend took me to Peterborough, where I boarded the *Royal Scot* for my trip to London. It was late in the afternoon when I got off the train at Paddington Station in London and stopped in a pub for a pint of ale served at room temperature. While I was standing at the bar, three coal miners came into the pub. They had coal dust all over their faces, hands, hair, and clothes. One of them came over to me and said, "Hi, Yank, buy you a beer?"

When I accepted, we introduced ourselves and he called his mates over to meet me. It was then that I noticed there were no other Yanks in the pub. Most Americans headed for Piccadilly Circus when they arrived in London. However, I enjoyed going to out-of-the-way places where I could meet English people that most Americans never got to meet. I learned that my new miner friends were Josh, Mick, and Henry.

While having our second beer, Josh said, "My mates bet me that a Yank wouldn't have anything to do with dirty old miners. That's why I came over to speak with you, and I won the bet."

"And I got a free beer," I said. They all got a big laugh out of my reply.

Noticing my wings, Mick asked, "What airplanes do you fly, Yank?"

"I'm a radar/navigator/bombardier on a B-17."

Josh shouted for everyone in the pub to hear, "A flying fortress bomber, he flies!"

Henry seemed to know a lot about the B-17 and said, "She's called the queen of the sky." Everyone agreed that she was, indeed, the queen of the sky.

We had a long conversation about the war and the suffering of the British people, especially the old people and the children.

When Henry asked what I thought about the war pact between America and the United Kingdom, my answer was, "From my study of history, England and America have had a close relationship for over one hundred years and I would expect nothing less than the friendly association and cooperation that we have today. My personal training is an example of the cooperation between our two countries. My rating in radar and navigation is a result of the training I received from RAF personnel at an RAF base."

Although my new friends told me they had not gone beyond the fourth and fifth grades in school, I found them to be very intelligent, caring, and thinking people.

Finally, Josh said, "We're getting too bloody serious. Let's play some darts." When Josh learned I had never played the game, he said, "Me and the Yank will take on you two and I'll teach him the fine art of darts." He did, too, because Henry and Mick only won one game out of the five we played—even with me as a millstone around Josh's neck. After each game, we would drink a toast to President Roosevelt and to King George.

It was finally time for us to part, since they would be later than usual getting home from the mine and I needed to leave for Hyde Park to get a room. As we were bidding each other "ta-ta," Josh gave me his telephone number and sincerely asked me to call him the next time I got to London. He wanted to have me out to his house for dinner and meet his family. I promised him I would do that.

Leaving the pub, I hopped on a big, red double-decker bus that took me to Hyde Park, where I got a room for the night at the Red Cross Club. Later, when I entered the dining room, I spotted Deke, a veteran bombardier from my squadron, sitting at a table alone. He saw me and motioned for me to join him. "I'm glad you're in town because I've been trying to make up my mind what to do tonight," he said.

After we had dinner, I called the girls Pete and I had dated the last time we were in London, but they were tied up for the evening. Deke and I decided to take in a movie at the Rialto and then hit a few pubs on the way back to the Red Cross Club. After leaving the last pub, we walked along, single-file, with our left hands barely touching the walls of buildings. That was the only way to walk at night in London because of the blackout. It was so black that it was impossible to see your own hand right up in your face. I heard Deke grunt as he bumped into someone, and then I saw the red tip of a burning cigarette. A female voice said, "Hi,

Yank, are you lonesome? I'll take it around the corner, standing up, for a pound-ten" (at that time, one pound, ten shillings was worth $6.30). Deke declined. We took a cab back to the Red Cross Club.

The next morning, I decided to go back to the base. Deke said, "I think I'll stay a couple of more days and make like a tourist in London." The *Royal Scot* took me back to Peterborough just in time for high tea. Having some time to kill before the bus arrived from the base, I stopped in the Idlewild Restaurant for tea and little sandwiches.

Back at the base, I went by the squadron bombardier's office to let Robbie know I had returned early.

"Man, I thought you would stay in London for three or four days," he said.

I replied, "I just got bored and thought I would get in some practice on the bomb trainer before my next mission."

"That's probably a good idea," he said, "because you're scheduled as the lead bombardier on the next mission."

Jokingly I asked, "What's the target?"

His reply was as expected, "You know I can't tell you that."

After having a cup of coffee with him, I headed for the O Club. I planned to hit the sack early since I would probably be on the bomb trainer most of the next day.

M/Sgt. Bob Traylor, the man in charge of the bomb trainer, and I first met when I was a cadet in Bombardier School. He was in charge of the bomb trainer at that school. Bob greeted me like a long-lost relative the next morning and said, "I'm sure glad to see they finally put bars on your shoulders. Everyone at the school heard about the raw deal you got at the graduation and how you later ripped off your wings and threw them away. We all wondered whatever happened to you."

It was easy for me to see that there wasn't going to be any training until Bob was brought up to date. I gave him a brief summary of all that had transpired since we last met and told him that I was now facing my eleventh mission. "Since I am scheduled as the squadron lead bombardier for the next mission, I felt it would be a good idea to get in some extra training time on the bomb trainer. And that is why I am here," I explained.

After I climbed up on the trainer, Bob started the terrain map of Germany moving below me and placed a metal, donut-shaped circle on the map to indicate the target. The trainer was set up on a bomb run, and I went through the usual bomb run procedures. I allowed the indices of the bombsight to meet, and the inked plunger at the bottom of the trainer zapped the paper map simulating the exact spot the bombs would hit. Bob yelled up at me, "You got a shack." The plunger had inked right in the middle of the donut Bob had placed on the map to represent the MPI (main point of impact).

After seven more bomb runs, all with good results, but no more shacks, Bob and I decided to go to the mess hall for lunch. On the way, I told him, "It sure is good to see you've added two rockers to your staff sergeant stripes. You must be doing something right."

"I sure hope so, because the extra money really comes in handy," he said. "My wife and I now have twin boys, that I haven't seen yet. They were born the week after I left for overseas."

After lunch we went back to the training building and I got in ten more practice runs. That gave me eighteen for the day—the most practice bomb runs I had ever tried in one day. After I climbed down off the trainer, and while Bob was adding up the scores, Robbie walked in and asked, "How'd he do?"

Bob gave him the thumbs-up sign and quipped, "Looks like he could be lead bombardier material."

Robbie replied, "Good thing, because he's flying squadron lead for tomorrow's mission. I've been assigned as deputy lead for the group, so I'll be up there watching him."

The three of us sat around drinking coffee for a while. Then Robbie, in a more serious tone, asked Bob, "Did you know your friend here shot down an enemy fighter with a nose gun last month?"

"No," Bob replied. "He forgot to tell me that, but he did say he went to gunnery school. Guess he learned pretty well there, just like he did in Bombardier's School."

My eleventh mission was back to Berlin. The crew I was assigned to had completed twenty-three missions. We were leading our squadron in the high box of the formation. All other bombardiers and toggleers in the high box would toggle their bombs when mine were dropped, using the bombsight. That really gave us a concentration of 500-pound bombs on the target. We were to use radar bombing techniques on that mission for better accuracy.

Our takeoff and forming up over King's Cliff went smoothly. We encountered no enemy fighter opposition, but the flak over the target was intense and accurate. The cloud cover over the target was like a solid sea of mashed potatoes, and if we had not been briefed for radar bombing we would have had to drop our bombs on an alternate target.

A new crew, on their first mission and flying in the tailend Charlie slot, was shot down over the target. We saw them go into a solid cloud bank but nothing else. They did not return from the mission.

Leaving the target area, we were really bounced around by the flak and received a considerable amount of damage to the aircraft. However, not one of our crew was injured. When we entered the landing pattern at Polebrook, there were numerous red flares being fired to indicate wounded on board quite a few aircraft.

After interrogation I headed for the O Club, where several of us usually gathered to hash over the mission. Robbie came in with a big smile and said, "Your practice on the bomb trainer yesterday was time well spent. The strike photos show the bombing accuracy for our squadron was excellent. Let me buy a beer for our new ace radar bombardier."

Mission number-twelve was to Merseburg, with another lead crew who had twenty-five missions to their credit. My job, again, was radar bombardier and we were assigned as the deputy lead for the squadron. We only spotted three enemy fighters, but they did not attack. Flak was meager and inaccurate. At interrogation we learned that the bombing was excellent, with the majority of the bombs falling in the center of the target area.

On my thirteenth mission, the target was Kiel. The crew I was assigned to was relatively new, with only three combat missions. Our aircraft had a bombsight and a black box (radar unit), and my instructions were to be prepared to use radar bombing techniques if we had bad weather over the target. Just prior to reaching the target area, we were told to swap places with the lead aircraft because he did not have radar, and weather reports indicated total cloud coverage in the target area. No enemy fighters were encountered, flak was very inaccurate, and bombing results were good. The trip home was very uneventful.

A third trip to Berlin became my fourteenth mission. This was briefed as an eight hour and fifteen minute mission, and my assignment was to evaluate the bombardier and the navigator to see if they were lead crew material or if they needed additional training. That meant I was the third man in the nose, and my seat for eight hours would be an upside-down ammunition box.

Sean, the navigator, had flown nine missions and David, the bombardier, had ten. The sheets for the evaluations that were handed to me prior to takeoff indicated that both men had been wounded on their last mission. It occurred to me that maybe what the brass was interested in was to determine if both men had become gun-shy after being wounded.

No enemy fighters came close to our formation, but flak over the target, as usual, was intense and accurate. Prior to reaching the target area, the lead ship for the group feathered an engine, surrendered the lead position to the deputy lead, and then fell farther back in the formation. He eventually dropped out of the formation and failed to return from the mission.

After completing the mission, I took the evaluation sheets over to squadron operations. Chuck, the squadron navigator, was in Robbie's office so I first discussed the evaluations with him. Chuck asked, "Did you detect any navigation errors or nervous problems during the mission?"

"Both men performed very well and neither displayed any extra nervousness caused by having been wounded."

Robbie came back to the office with coffee for all of us and I repeated the same thing to him. We talked about combat in general and I stated, "I don't know about you guys, but I am nervous on every mission until I get into the area where all of my effort has to be devoted to bombing, navigation, radar, or any combination of the three." We all agreed that most people do experience fear on a combat mission.

A short time later, Chuck said, "Tell me something, Bill, with all of your training, how come you're still a lieutenant? Did you screw up somewhere?"

"I guess I did—somewhere," I replied.

Robbie told the whole story to Chuck, who then said to me, "You mean you went through all of the hell of the Cadet Program without getting a commission and then you threw away your wings?"

I just said, "Guilty."

Robbie said that Chuck flew two missions with Clark Gable and then told Chuck, "Bill taught Clark Gable in Gunnery School and had the honor of pinning on his gunner wings." As we were leaving the office, Robbie told Chuck, "Bill's a pretty good gunner himself. He shot down an Me 109 with a nose gun last month."

Chuck shook his head and said, "And he's still just a lieutenant?"

June 6, 1944, was the day of my fifteenth mission, the crew's fifth. We went to Caen, France. My assignment with that new crew was to be their navigator and also to check out the bombardier because he was having considerable trouble getting his bombs on the target. On the last three missions, George, the bombardier, had missed the target completely. George was aware of my job on the mission, and he acted very nervous every time I asked him a question or tried to engage him in a little small talk. I finally said, "George, this is not the Cadet Program and I am not along to wash you out, only to help you identify the problem you are having."

Getting it out in the open seemed to help him and he told me, "I have tried retracing every step but it has not helped me identify my problem. So I sure hope you can find what I have been doing wrong."

I told him that I would stay back out of his way and follow through on the procedures, to see if we could identify the problem. George agreed and started by checking the twelve 500-pound bombs in the bomb bay, arming wires, safety pins, etc.

We then both swung ourselves up into the front escape hatch of the aircraft and strapped ourselves in our seats for the takeoff. We were the number-three ship in the low box. Flying in that position did not require a lot of work on the part of the navigator, but I always did my flight planning as though we would be in the air all alone. I had finished most of my flight planning after the regular briefing. We encountered no enemy fighters, and the flak was moderate but inaccurate.

During the bomb run I stood behind George, watching his every move. From my position, the problem was quickly very obvious because George kept lifting his head from the bombsight to look at the flak. After the bombs dropped and George closed the bomb bay doors, I asked, "George, did the strike photos from previous missions indicate your bombs were dropping prior to target area?"

He thought for a moment and then said, "Yes, but how did you know and what was the reason?"

"You were so worried about the flak that you kept lifting your head from the bombsight to see how close the flak was getting," I told him.

George admitted, "I was worried about the flak but I didn't think I raised my head that much."

"That was a one-and-three-quarter-minute bomb run, and you looked up from the bombsight fourteen times. That small distraction caused you to not keep the indices in the bombsight apart long enough. The indices coming together too soon allowed the bombs to drop prematurely and strike the ground prior to reaching the target. George, whenever you see the black puff of the flak, it has been preceded by the bursting of the anti-aircraft shell which already expelled the steel pieces that we call flak. So, when you see the black puff, it is too late to worry because it has either hit you or missed you. If it missed you, you have nothing to worry about and if it hit you, you still have nothing to worry about, ever again. The Norden bombsight is an excellent weapon but it is stupid; it needs you to tell it what to do. So keep your eye glued to the eyepiece of your bombsight from the time you start the bomb run until it is time for you to allow the indices to come together so the bombs will leave the bomb bay."

A load seemed to be lifted from George's shoulders. He said, "I wish you could have gone with me on my first combat mission."

"I'm just glad we have your problem solved. Now you take it from here and put those bombs on the target."

This uneventful trip turned out to be a good day to check out a new bombardier who was dropping short of the target. Our main purpose was to have our bombs make foxholes for our ground troops, who were invading the continent of Europe. The day was D-Day.

CHAPTER 10

After D-Day

Mission number-sixteen was to Le Bourget airfield in France, with another new crew from the States. One complete combat wing, led by Lieutenant Colonel Ball, attacked the target. I was assigned as the bombardier for a crew with three missions completed. We saw about thirty enemy fighters in the area of our formation, but they did not attack. Three B-17s were lost to flak which was intense as well as accurate in the target area. Our aircraft received some battle damage, and both waist gunners were slightly wounded.

The return trip to our base was uneventful. Upon landing, both wounded gunners were taken to the hospital, patched up, and released. When the interrogation period was over, we all headed for the combat crew mess hall for dinner and then to the armament shack to clean our guns.

Hamburg was my seventeenth combat mission, and my position with a new crew was radar/bombardier. The crew had just arrived in England and was flying mission number-one. It was easy to see they were excited and nervous at the same time. Our position in the formation was tailend Charlie, the last plane in the low box, which was the usual position for new crews. We did not have any fighter opposition, but flak at the target was intense and very accurate.

Back to Hamburg for mission number-eighteen in my quest for a complete combat tour. My crew for that day had experience, with fourteen combat missions. I was assigned as the eleventh man on the crew, at the Mickey operator position next to the radio operator. Other than the usual intense and accurate flak in the target area, the mission and our return to Polebrook was almost routine.

Over a beer at the O Club, Robbie informed me that our squadron was to stand down for maintenance for a few days. He said, "If you have anybody to see in London, you might as well take off for a few days. I'd like to go with you, but the old man wants me here during the maintenance stand down, in case there is any problem with bombsights."

After arriving in London on a Saturday morning, I went to a phone booth and telephoned Josh, the coal miner I had befriended earlier. When he answered the phone, I started to explain who I was but he interrupted me. "Hey, Bill, you're the only Yank I know! Sure I remember you." When I told him what train station I was calling from he told me, "You're only fifteen minutes from my house. Just have a cabby bring you here." He gave me his address and then said, "Min and I won't hear of you staying anywhere but with us, so just come directly here."

I hailed a taxi and shortly we approached a row of small homes with thatched roofs. There was Josh, standing at the curb watching for me. He greeted me like an old friend.

The first thing he said was, "You really surprised me because I had no idea I would ever see you again or that you would even call. When I told some of my mates at the mine that I had played darts with a Yank, they didn't believe me because they said all the bloody Yanks want to do is get drunk and chase women."

Josh grabbed my B-4 bag and we went into his house. Once inside, he introduced me to his wife, Min, his eleven-year-old daughter, Annie, and his nine-year-old son, Mark. Min greeted me with a sweet smile, but the kids just stood back and stared at me until Josh sent them out in the backyard to play.

"I hope you will excuse the kids," said Josh. "They've never seen a Yank up close."

"The kids probably feel like I do," I replied. "Whenever I go to a zoo and see a new animal, I also stare."

With that, Min and Josh really broke up with laughter. Min showed me upstairs to the guest room.

When I came back downstairs, Josh was sitting in his chair, smoking a pipe. I went back up to get my pipe and tobacco. Min joined us in the living room and we engaged in small talk while dinner was cooking. When I learned they were both from Ireland, I told them that my mother's parents and my father's grandparents went to America from County Cork. They said in unison, "That's where we are from."

Min asked many questions about America, and I tried to give her straight answers. When I told her I was born and raised in the suburb of Hyde Park, in Cincinnati, Ohio, she said, "Oh, just like Hyde Park in London." She then brought out Annie's geography book and I pointed out to her where Cincinnati was located, as well as some other places she asked about.

When Min got up to check on dinner, Josh whispered to me, "Her name is Minerva but she hates the name so I call her Min."

"Josh," I said, "she is a lovely lady and I promise not to call her Minerva."

We chuckled about that as I filled my pipe from my tobacco pouch. Josh seemed to be fascinated by the small zippered leather pouch and the smell of my tobacco. I offered him a pipeful and told him it was an American tobacco called Prince Albert. I put the pouch on the table and invited him to help himself, as I had more upstairs in my B-4 bag.

Min called the kids in to clean up for dinner and advised us that food would be on the table in ten minutes. I followed Josh to the back porch, where we both washed up at a sink there. The aroma from the Irish stew and newly baked bread that Min had prepared made my mouth water. She had also made a fresh salad from her backyard garden.

The kids came to the table and, now less shy, wanted to sit next to me. Josh said the blessing and we all dug in to the wonderful dinner Min had prepared.

When Min went to the kitchen to get the dessert, I asked Annie what subjects she liked the most in school. She immediately replied, "Geography, spelling, and homemaking." Mark told me his favorite was summer vacation.

We all laughed at his remark, and then he asked me, "Are you a flier?" When I told him yes, he said, "When I grow up I want to become a flier so I can fight for my country like you are doing."

I took off my wings, pinned them on Mark's shirt, and told him, "Maybe that will help you keep your mind on your goal." I whispered to Annie, "I have another pair of wings up in my bag that I will get for you after dinner." I then turned to Mark and said, "Mark, I'm amazed that you have such mature thoughts. But I want you to know, I'm not just fighting for my country. I'm also fighting for your country and for all people who love freedom like we do. I hope that when you and others your age begin to fly that it will be for fun and not for war."

Josh said simply, "Amen."

When Min came in with a beautiful rhubarb pie, she asked, "What's everyone so serious about?"

Mark rushed over to show her his wings and Annie told her mother, "I shall have a pair also in a little while."

When I told Min about Mark's comment, she said, "He gets his ideas from his dad because Josh served in tanks with General Montgomery in Africa until he was wounded."

When dinner was over, I told Min that I had never eaten such delicious Irish stew and that rhubarb pie has always been a favorite of mine. I then went upstairs to get another pair of wings for Annie. Both kids wanted to go outside to show their new wings to their friends in the neighborhood. Josh told them, "Be in by 8:30." Both kids took off flying out the door.

Josh and I cleared the table while Min washed dishes. We all three dried the dishes and Min put them away. When I brought down my ditty bag, in which I kept my smoking material, Josh and I sat at the table to clean our pipes. He pulled a straw out of the broom and ran it through the stem of his pipe. I tossed him a package of pipe cleaners, and it was obvious he had never used or seen such things. He was curious about what I had in my ditty bag, so I dumped it out on the table to show him what I carried in my smoking bag.

Another trip upstairs to my B-4 bag and I brought down the pound box of chocolate-covered cherries I had brought for Min and six candy bars each for the kids. Min cried because it had been so long since she had had any "sweets." She told me that she would ration the candy bars to the kids. Then I gave Josh three unopened tins of Prince Albert and two new packs of pipe cleaners. It was very difficult for me to realize how much those simple gifts meant to my new friends.

When Annie and Mark returned, Annie was fascinated with the dirty pipe cleaners her father and I used to clean our pipes. She asked if she could have them. When I asked why she would want those dirty things, she said, "So I can wash them and use them to roll my hair." I gave her two new packs of cleaners and told her, "Now you won't have to fool with those old dirty pipe cleaners." Min gave each of the kids half of a candy bar and their eyes brightened as they bit into that Milky Way. When they smiled at the sweet taste, the caramel could be seen clinging to their teeth.

After the kids went to bed, we three talked until it was time for Josh to leave for his night shift at the mine. As Josh and I were saying "ta-ta" he hugged me and whispered, "You will always be welcome in my house. But if we don't get to see each other again, I will pray for your safe return to your family." Min walked with Josh to the train, and I went upstairs to retire.

The next morning, Min fixed a fine breakfast for all of us and I told her how much I appreciated their kind hospitality. As I was saying goodbye to the kids, I noticed that Mark was about to cry. I said to him, "Mark, always keep your goal in front of you—and learn to fly for fun." Both kids thanked me for the wings and the candy. I telephoned for a taxi and headed for the train that would take me back to war.

It would have been better for me if I had stayed in London a little longer because the maintenance stand down was over when I returned to the base. My nineteenth mission was to hit the aircraft plant at Leipzig and my assignment was to another new crew from the States. Their regular bombardier was sick with the flu. It was another tailend Charlie mission, last ship in the low box—the ship the German fighters went after first.

That day we had no enemy fighters but very intense and accurate flak. We had a long, two-minute-and-25-second bomb run, during which time the flak bursts bounced us all over the sky. My bombs fell into the smoke and flames of the previous bomb drops. Just after I closed the bomb bay doors, we received a direct hit in the radio room and the radio operator, a nice kid from Iowa, who was only nineteen years old, was killed. Nine other aircraft were damaged as they left the target area. Our hydraulic system was shot away by flak, and we were deep in Nazi Germany.

We climbed a little so that other ships in our formation could inspect the underside of our aircraft. We were told the bottom of our ship was riddled with flak holes and one of the landing gear doors had been shot away. All that remained of the tire on that wheel was flapping strands of rubber. That meant a wheels-up landing, assuming we made it back to the base. Luckily, we were able to keep up with the formation and the engines seemed to perform well.

Leaving the target area, we got too close to Merseburg and sustained more flak damage to the tail section. The pilot called me on the intercom and asked me to go to the tail and check on the tail gunner. John, the navigator said, "I'll take care of your nose gun if we get jumped by enemy fighters."

Getting unhooked from my oxygen line and my communication line and out of my flak suit took some doing because the flak was still bouncing us around the sky. Unhooking one D ring on my parachute, I tucked the parachute under my left arm, plugged my oxygen mask into a walk-around bottle, and made my way through the bomb bay into the radio room. I passed the dead radio operator and entered the waist section. Both waist gunners were OK but very frightened because the radio operator had been killed. The tail gunner had been wounded, but not seriously, so I broke open the first aid kit and treated the wound on the back of his right hand. The flak that wounded his hand had also torn off his glove. After I bandaged his hand I told him, "Just keep your hand inside your heavy flying suit and you'll be all right until the real medics can do a better job on the wound."

His reply was, "You did a real good doctoring job, Lieutenant, and I thank you for coming all the way back here to help me."

Reversing my route, I stopped in the waist section to talk with the two waist gunners. When I asked them if they were worried when all that flak was bursting around us, in unison they said, "I sure was." I said, "Me too. You guys should sit up in the plexiglas nose and watch it bursting from all directions. I get scared on every mission. But when I concentrate on the job I have to do, the scared feeling goes away."

My walk-around bottle was getting low, so I headed for the cockpit. Going into the radio room, I looked back at the waist gunners. They both smiled and gave me the thumbs-up sign. When I reached the cockpit, I told the pilot what I had found in the radio room, the waist section, and the tail section. He said, "Sure thank you for looking after my gunners."

After we crossed the coast of England, the pilot announced on the intercom that our hydraulic system was gone and one tire on the landing gear had been blown away. Consequently, he would get over the field and give the crew the option of a bailout or a wheels-up landing. The flight engineer said, "I took off with you and I'll land with you." The rest of us all agreed to do the same.

The pilot let the tower know about our damage and that we would be making a wheels-up landing in the grass next to the runway. They responded with, "Roger, you are number-one for a straight-in approach. All other returning aircraft, take up a racetrack pattern over the field and watch for aircraft making wheels-up landing."

John and I left the nose and braced ourselves against the bulkhead just aft of the radio room with the two waist gunners. The pilot held the aircraft off as long as possible as the firetrucks raced along the runway beside us. He then made a very good wheels-up landing. By the time we stopped throwing up dirt and grass, the firetrucks were all around the aircraft and the medics were waiting for our dead and wounded. The rest of us hopped on a 6X6 truck for a ride to interrogation.

After a long interrogation, Robbie and Major Ledoux sent word they wanted to see me at Squadron Operations. When I entered the office they both wanted to know if I was all right. I said, "Sure, I'm indestructible."

Robbie said, "I'm glad you're OK because I really need you again tomorrow."

We had a couple of cups of coffee while we hashed over the intense flak we ran into over Leipzig. Afterwards we went to the combat crew mess hall, then I headed for a cold shower and my bed.

No day off after my second crash landing, so mission number-twenty was to Munich to hit the airfield. My crew that day had completed twelve combat missions and they were a lead crew. My assignment was as the lead bombardier for the high box. Major Ledoux was leading the squadron on this one, with Robbie as his bombardier. The bombardier in each lead plane in the formation used radar bombing techniques, and all other bombardiers and toggleers salvoed their bombs when they saw the bombs drop from the lead ship. No enemy fighters were seen. Several ships in the formation received flak damage, but we didn't. The flight back to the base was uneventful.

After interrogation, I met Major Ledoux and Robbie at the air crew mess hall and learned they had received severe flak damage to their aircraft but no injuries to the crew. As we were having a second cup of coffee, Major Ledoux whispered to me, "We have to go back tomorrow. Can you hack two days in a row?"

"Major, I'll go anywhere you want me to go, at anytime, as long as it's in a B-17," was my answer.

After leaving the mess hall, we all headed for bed because we knew tomorrow would be another rough one.

My twenty-first mission was back to Munich for another try

at the airfield with the same crew and the same position in the formation. Again, no enemy fighters but intense and accurate flak over the target.

On the bomb run, one aircraft in our formation was hit by flak and set on fire. As it went into a shallow dive, several parachutes were seen but the aircraft blew up when it hit the ground.

Back at the base, during interrogation, we learned that nine of the twelve aircraft in our formation received flak damage over Munich but injuries were light. It was obvious during the interrogation that we had some very tired combat crews in the room. Later, while sitting in the mess hall with my crew for that day, I saw Robbie motioning for me to come over to his table, where he was sitting alone. Excusing myself, I picked up my tray and joined him. After I sat down, his first words were, "How do you feel?"

"OK, but dog tired."

"We have to go back to Munich again tomorrow and I just don't have enough lead bombardiers."

I put my head down on the table because I knew what was coming next. Robbie said, "I hate to ask you to fly three consecutive days, especially to a place like Munich, but I am really hurting for lead bombardiers. Major Roper will be leading an eighteen-ship formation tomorrow. I'll be flying as his bombardier, and I desperately need you as the lead bombardier in the high box."

I looked back up and told him, "Robbie, if an old guy of twenty-six years like you is able to fly two consecutive combat missions to Munich, I guess a young guy of twenty years like me can fly three." When our coffee was gone, I suggested, "Maybe we should both hit the sack early tonight."

"Right you are, ole buddy," he replied. "See you in the morning."

Wake-up time came too quickly. Still half asleep, I headed for the cold shower house out back in the hopes that it would pep me up a little for my twenty-second mission. It pepped me up all right; nearly blue from the cold water, I didn't stay in it long. Breakfast was the usual meal before a combat mission: pancakes, syrup, fresh egg on top, and fresh milk.

At briefing, there were people present who had been at one of the other Munich briefings. Thus I was not the only one who would get missions to Munich on consecutive days. My crew for the day was a lead crew with twelve missions under their belt. We introduced ourselves after the briefing and headed for the armament shack to pick up our guns, then to the aircraft.

Swinging up into the aircraft by way of the nose escape hatch, I worked my way back to a position between the bomb racks to check my load. The twelve 500-pound bombs were snug in the bomb bay with arming wires all in place, so I headed to my office in the nose. Ken, the navigator, was hard at work on his maps and charts. Looking up, he said, "My pilot tells me you're a navigator as well as a bombardier."

"Yes," I said, "plus Mickey operator and aerial gunner."

Ken then asked, "When in the hell did you have time to get all of that training and still fly twenty-one missions?"

I told him about my hospital stay and the flight surgeon not wanting me to fly at high altitude until he was sure the sinus operation was a success, and the opportunity I had to go to an RAF school.

The pilot came on the intercom and advised everyone we were next in line for takeoff. Almost immediately, we received the green flare and started our takeoff roll. We climbed at 300 feet per minute until we reached 13,000 feet. Meeting up with the rest of the formation over "The Wash," we headed for Munich.

The route to the target was unhindered and we gradually climbed to our bombing altitude of 28,000 feet. We did see about twenty-five or thirty FW 190s and Me 109s, but they didn't attack.

Ken said, "It doesn't look like you'll add another Me 109 notch to your gun today." When I asked how he knew I got credit for one of them, he replied, "Bill, all the gunners on the base know you graduated from Gunnery School and that you shot down an enemy fighter with a flexible nose gun. Most of them even know the date—April 13, wasn't it?"

"Ken," I said, "I honestly don't remember the date because it was just something I had to do because those bastard Germans were making a company front attack and shooting at me with headlight tracers."

"Take my word, it was 13 April."

On the intercom Ken called, "Navigator to pilot, we are ten minutes from the IP [the initial point]."

The pilot answered, "Roger. Bombardier, are you ready to fly the airplane?"

"Roger," I replied.

Just prior to the IP, the call came, "Pilot to bombardier, turning on the PPI, the ship is all yours."

"Roger, I've got it."

This was to be a two-minute bomb run and we were really being tossed around by flak bursts. The indices of my bombsight came together, and I watched the red lights on my bomb panel go out one by one. Each light going out indicated a 500-pound bomb heading for Germany. When the last one went out, I hit the salvo switch and announced, "Bombardier to pilot, bombs away. Let's go home."

He came back, "Roger, we're on the way."

I asked the radio operator to make sure the bomb racks were clear before I closed the bomb bay doors. He called back with, "Bomb bay clear."

"Roger," I said, and closed the bomb bay doors.

The pilot broke in, "Pilot to crew, we took some hard flak hits over the target and I think our whole hydraulic system is gone. When we get back to the base, we could crank the gear down by hand but we still would not have any brakes. I'll keep you all informed."

We had no further trouble on the trip home, but when we got in the traffic pattern at the base there was very heavy rain. We learned that one aircraft landed too far down the runway, ran off the end, and crashed through the hedge and barbed wire entanglements that marked the perimeter of the base. A few minutes later, another plane did the same thing. Before we entered the traffic pattern, the pilot advised the control tower that we had no hydraulics and we were going to land at Molesworth Airfield because of the long grass strip at the end of their runway. The control tower answered, "Roger, and good luck, guys."

Over Molesworth, the pilot advised their control tower of our hydraulic problem and that when we cranked the gear down by hand we did not get a green light for down and locked. The control tower advised us that the grass overrun at the end of the runway was 8,000 feet long and recommended a wheels-up landing on it. Ken and I headed for the waist section and braced ourselves against the bulkheads along with the two waist gunners.

The pilot didn't allow the aircraft to settle in until we were over the grass overrun. We used up a lot of that overrun, even with a wheels-up landing. The firetrucks and the "meat wagon" followed us down the runway but, thank God, were not needed. We were all taken to the base hospital and checked over. The 303rd Bomb Group intelligence people came to the hospital and prepared our interrogation reports on the mission. They then gave the pilot copies of the reports to take back to the 351st Bomb Group Intelligence Office.

The medics released us and we walked to the entrance of the hospital, discussing how we would get back to Polebrook. Four staff cars pulled up in front. One was driven by Maj. Paul Fishburne, the new 509th Bomb Squadron CO, and another was driven by the squadron bombardier, Capt. "Robbie" Robinson. The other two vehicles were driven by other combat crew members who volunteered to take us home. They all came running over to us, asking if we were all right.

Robbie grabbed my hand and laughingly said, "You dumb jerk, why did you agree to fly to Munich on three consecutive days?"

"Because you told me you needed help," I replied.

In a more serious tone he asked me, "Are you OK?"

"Sure," I said, "but I'm going to make a recommendation that crash landings be limited to one per combat tour."

With a smile he said, "I'll be sure to endorse your recommendation. How many does that make for you?"

"Three," I answered, "but I'm not trying for any record."

We all climbed into the staff cars and I slept all the way back to our base. When we arrived, I awoke refreshed and headed for the O Club to have a couple of beers before turning in for the night.

Peenemunde was mission twenty-three. That was the area for German rocket experimentation and the launch area for many of the V-1 and V-2 rockets that had been raining such hell and destruction on English cities. Major Roper was leading a thirty-six plane attack on the target, and I was back at the tailend Charlie position again with another new crew as their bombardier. On that mission, I toggled out my bombs when the lead bombardier in the low box dropped his load. We saw no enemy fighters and flak was very inaccurate. That was a very puzzling situation, when one considered the importance of that area to Germany's buzz-bomb efforts. Compared to almost any of my other missions, that was a real milk run.

The return home and the short interrogation were routine. As we were removing and cleaning our weapons after the interrogation, this new crew had many questions about the flak and fighter opposition we encountered over Germany. I tried to answer their questions without a lot of embellishment or gory details about B-17s going down in flames, but at the same time I realized it was not fair to a new crew to make it sound as if there was no risk or danger. They asked me to describe some of my missions. Believing that my missions had been rather typical of what others had gone through, I started with mission number-one and got up to number-eight before getting tired of hearing myself talk. Soon I was headed for the O Club before turning in for the night.

For my twenty-fourth combat mission, we went to Schweinfurt to hit the V.K.F. ball-bearing plant, a vital industry for Germany's war effort. We were told at the briefing that next to the coal and steel of the Ruhr Valley, ball bearings were the most valuable product of the German war production. Major Roper led two twelve-ship boxes to that target, with Robbie as his bombardier. My assignment was the bombardier position for a crew flying their thirty-fifth and last combat mission. They were a lead crew, and that was our position in the high box. We were extremely fortunate not to have received any major flak damage to our plane, as four ships in our formation went down in flames due to flak.

Bombing accuracy was good and there were several secondary explosions in the target area. The trip home was without any problems.

Over the field the pilot announced on the intercom, "Is everybody ready for our victory pass over the field?" One by one we all answered with an emphatic, "Roger!" Sitting on my little bombardier's seat, I tightened my seat belt as we made our approach at full power and dropped lower and lower and lower. When we crossed the end of the runway, where most pilots try to touch down, we were so low that, if our landing gear had been down, we would have been rolling along the runway. Through the plexiglas nose I had a complete view of what was going on. Exhilaration is the only way to explain my feeling. The pilot held the ship at that altitude the entire length of the runway. Reaching the end of the runway, he pulled back on the yoke, kicked in a little left rudder, and made a graceful climbing turn away from the field.

The control tower called on the radio and said, "That was a beautiful victory pass. You are number-one to land."

The pilot replied, "Roger, and thank you, tower, for always being there when we needed you."

Our landing was on the very first part of the runway—a textbook, three-point landing. What an ending to a successful thirty-five-mission combat tour by a great bunch of guys. And I had the honor of sharing their glorious moment.

Thirty-six aircraft in three twelve-ship boxes, led by Major Richardson, became my twenty-fifth combat mission. Our destination was Merseberg. My job on this one was bombardier for a crew with eighteen missions completed. The mission was rather routine, even though we were jumped by fifteen FW 190s and Me 109s. They made two passes at the formation and then left the area. Flak in the target area was moderate to very heavy, but we did not sustain any damage. The return to base was without incident.

My next combat mission was back to Merseberg. Colonel Burns led a thirty-six-plane raid, and I was assigned to another veteran crew with twenty missions to their credit. Their aircraft was a new B-17G, with a chin turret. Since I had put myself through several practice sessions with the chin turret, I was really glad to have a chance to try it in combat.

Only four Me 109s hit our formation. They made one pass and departed, but I got off several rounds at them. Then the flak started. It was very intense and accurate – much different from what hit us the previous day. One aircraft in the high box was hit and exploded in midair. Several other ships received severe damage, but ours received only minor damage and no injuries. Thirty-six aircraft left the field that morning; only thirty-two returned. One aircraft crashed on landing because of brake failure.

After interrogation, the clerk from my squadron told me the CO would like to see me for a few minutes. Major Fishburne, our new CO, and I had flown together a couple of times while he was still a captain.

When I reported to him, he came from behind his desk to shake hands and said, "Bill, I haven't seen you since your crash landing at Molesworth."

"It sure does seem like a long time ago since that night," I said, "and longer still since our mission to Berlin. I haven't had a chance to offer you congratulations on your promotion." He thanked me and told me to have a seat. We talked about the new B-17s with the chin turrets and I told him, "I had the opportunity to fly in one on my mission today, to Merseberg. I fired the guns when we entered enemy territory and searched the sky with the new gunsight. It seems to be a fine new weapon, and I'm anxious to use it to really engage some enemy fighters."

"I see that you have been flying every other day and sometimes every day lately," the major said.

"Yes sir," I replied. "It's my understanding that we have a shortage of people with my ratings. And besides, the more I fly, the sooner I get in my thirty-five missions and go home."

He then told me, "You have been personally invited to attend a two-week update on radar techniques at the RAF school near Dover."

"Major," I said, "I have nine more missions to go to finish my combat tour and two weeks is probably all that will be needed to finish."

"Bill, you have been pushing yourself too hard and I think you could use some time away from combat," he said. "Besides that, with the new radar techniques your last nine missions could be more meaningful."

After a lengthy discussion, it was finally decided I would leave the next day for RAF Hawkinge to attend a two-week updated course.

As with my first course at RAF Hawkinge, the instruction was excellent and the topics were the very latest. Ten and twelve hours per day seemed to be the norm for RAF schools. I probably would have gotten more rest flying combat missions.

Back at Polebrook, my twenty-seventh mission was to Ludwigshafen with a crew that had flown eighteen combat missions without an injury. My position was radar/bombardier, and we were the lead ship in the high box. No enemy fighters were seen, but the flak over the target was very intense. The results of our bombing by radar were unobserved due to smoke and haze in the target area; however, later reports indicated the bombing was excellent.

One of our new aircraft, a B-17G, was shot down just southwest of the target, near Saarbrucken. Another of our aircraft, with two badly damaged engines, was forced to crash land near Paris. Two other aircraft were also shot down by flak on that mission. Our ship took several flak hits but nothing serious.

Even though I was in a G model, I still did not get to engage the enemy with the two guns in the chin turret. We had a smooth return to the base.

The target of my next mission was Plauen. My crew for the day was a lead crew that had completed twelve missions. We were flying deputy lead in the high box, and our aircraft was one of the

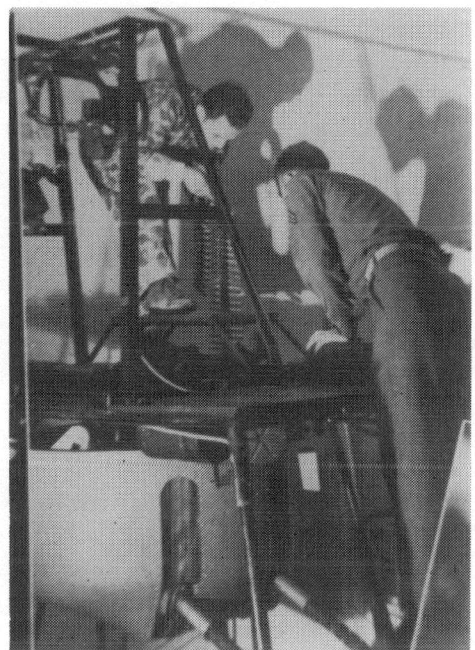

Chin turret trainer

new B-17Gs with a chin turret. Flak was ineffective and light but the Luftwaffe was really up in force. After dropping my bombs, I pulled the gunsight and trigger for the chin turret over into position just as we were jumped by about fifty enemy fighters. They were mostly Me 109s and FW 190s attacking in pairs. This was my first real chance to use the chin turret in a fight.

The gunners were calling out fighters coming in on our formation: "Bogey at nine o'clock," "Me 109 at six o'clock," "FW 190 doing slow roll attacking tail section from above."

I was scanning the sky with my gunsight and the last sighting caused me to slightly depress my trigger. From that attitude of attack, the enemy aircraft could roll up in front of us, and that is what he did. Just as I pulled the trigger, pouring hundreds of rounds of .50-caliber ammunition out in front of our aircraft, that FW 190 rolled up into my line of fire. I saw my tracers going into the rear end and right wing of that enemy airplane. He pulled up, dumped his canopy, and bailed out. The aircraft nosed over and headed for the ground, and we could see the pilot floating down in his parachute.

Kevin, the navigator, was yelling excitedly at the top of his voice, "You got him . . . you got him! You hit the son-of-a-bitch and he bailed out." The pilot and co-pilot yelled down from the cockpit, "Great shooting!" The enemy fighters must have been running low on fuel because they broke off the attack and left the area.

A couple of the gunners came up to the nose and pounded me on the back. Another one started up to the nose, but the pilot called on the intercom, "Gunners, get back to your positions. We are still in enemy territory. You can congratulate your fellow gunner when we get back home."

Six B-17s were shot down by the enemy fighters in the target area that day. Another aircraft was badly damaged by fighters but made it to Belgium, where he crash landed.

The trip back home was almost quiet, except for the gunners' chatter about painting a swastika on the nose of their aircraft. After we landed and got parked in our revetment area, Kevin and I gathered up our maps, charts, and other equipment and dropped down from the nose escape hatch to find all of the gunners waiting there. Every one of them had to shake my hand and pound me on the back. I began to feel like a halfback who had taken a pass in for a touchdown, untouched by the opposition but beaten down to the ground by his own team. It was a great feeling, though, and I joined the joyous celebration in the "end zone," our revetment.

After interrogation, I was standing around talking with our gunners when Robbie walked over, grabbed me by the shoulders, and said, "You son-of-a-gun, you did it again. This time it's the first enemy fighter shot down with a chin turret in our squadron." I asked one of the interrogators how many enemy fighters we got that day, and he replied, "Six, but yours was the only one from a chin turret."

Soon afterward, I headed for the O Club with Robbie. He and all the bombardiers at the bar bought me drinks the rest of the evening.

My goal was getting closer. Combat mission twenty-nine for me was to Frankfurt with a new crew from the States. This was to be their first taste of combat. The pilot had to chase the gunners back to their own positions because they wanted to ask me how I shot down two enemy fighters. He could tell it was very difficult for me to answer their questions while getting my nose gun mounted before we were told to taxi out for takeoff.

From the time we left Polebrook until we returned, it was another milk run – no fighters and only one moderate flak barrage over the target.

Our trip back home and our landing were routine. When we walked into the interrogation room, one of the intelligence people yelled at me, "Hey, Lieutenant, did you get any enemy aircraft today?"

I yelled back at him, "No – and no one else did either because the Germans hid their fighters when they learned the 351st Bomb Group would be in the area."

Cologne was combat mission number-thirty. My crew for the day was a lead crew with twenty-one missions without a wounded crew member and no serious damage to their aircraft. They had just been assigned a new B-17G.

Duke, a card-playing friend, was the co-pilot on the crew and we had a lot of fun joking with each other. That was our first time to fly together. When I told him that this one was thirty for me, he said, "Man, I wish I had thirty. I enjoy what I'm doing, but I sure will be glad to go home."

I agreed and told him, "That's the reason I offer to fly with anyone who needs a fill-in for a missing crew member."

The tower gave us the green flare and we started our takeoff roll. We joined up with our formation at The Wash and headed for Germany. We were the lead ship in the low box, and the tail gunner reported to the pilot that we had a real good, tight formation. The navigator gave the pilot a position report and the pilot got on the intercom, "Pilot to gunners, we are over enemy territory. Test fire your guns with short bursts. That goes for our ace gunner in the nose also." That started the gunners with lines of comic relief: "Hey ace, are you going to leave any for us? What do you load your guns with, ace?"

We saw no enemy fighters that day and the flak was ineffective, except for a round that penetrated one aircraft's ball turret and exploded. The ball turret was blown completely away, and a large hole was made in the side of the fuselage. The radio operator and the ball turret gunner were both blown out of the aircraft. The pilot and co-pilot somehow took that ship home and landed safely with the rest of the crew uninjured.

Our return to the base was without any problems. After interrogation, Duke said, "I'll help you clean your guns because I've always wanted to handle a machine gun." Duke did a good job after I taught him how to field strip a .50-caliber machine gun.

We placed the guns in the rack and headed for the combat crew mess. The whole crew was there and the gunners wanted to know if Duke's helping me clean my guns meant that he would help them do the same thing. "When one of you guys shoots down a Kraut fighter," he quipped, "I'll clean your guns for you – and that's a promise."

My thirty-first mission was to Magdeburg with another replacement crew from the States. They had been on five practice missions, but no combat missions. I was to give their bombardier a check ride to determine his procedures, so I filled in as the navigator. Since we were assigned to the tailend Charlie position, there was not much navigation to do unless we got lost from the formation. We saw no enemy fighters, but the flak was moderate and accurate. One aircraft lost three engines over the target and crash landed near the coast. The crew was returned to the base safely but not the aircraft.

The bombardier's procedures were fine and he was cool and professional when the flak started. I did not write it up, but I did have one suggestion for him. "Jim, it's not required 'in the book' but I make it a practice, after I announce bombs away, to hit the salvo switch and have the radio operator check the bomb bay before closing the bomb bay doors. By doing that the bomb bay doors are not closed on a bomb hung up in the bomb bay."

Jim replied, "I appreciate the suggestion and I'll start using that procedure. I'd hate to carry a live bomb back to the base, especially if we had to make a crash landing."

Kassel was number thirty-two for me. I was sure getting close to that magic number of thirty-five. On that mission my job was at the radar/bombardier position on a lead crew with nineteen combat missions completed. We flew in the deputy lead position for the high box in a new B-17G. We started out with thirty-seven aircraft, but two had to abort before reaching the target due to mechanical problems. No enemy aircraft were seen; however, flak was intense and continuous in the target area. That caused serious damage to fourteen aircraft. The return to the base was without a problem.

The marshaling yard at Nurnburg became mission number thirty-three for me. I was the Mickey operator (radar) in the radio room. No enemy fighters were seen; flak in the target area was moderate and accurate. Nine aircraft were damaged by the flak, one so badly that he had to crash land in enemy territory. We received considerable damage to the aircraft from a flak burst just under the nose. The bombardier was hit, but his wounds were not life-threatening. I said a prayer of thanksgiving because if their bombardier had not come back from leave a day early, I would have taken his place in the nose. Luck of the Irish – or destiny?

When we entered the landing pattern, the co-pilot fired a red flare to alert the medics that we had wounded on board. After the long interrogation and then dinner, I headed for the O Club for some "hangar flying" with friends.

Another marshaling yard became mission number thirty-four, this time at Cologne. My job was bombardier for another new crew, and we flew in the tailend Charlie slot. Although the flak at the target was very heavy and accurate, no aircraft were damaged. One aircraft had to land at Brussels to obtain fuel, but it returned to Polebrook the next day.

All the way back to base, the same thought kept repeating itself in my brain: one more mission, one more mission. That night at the O Club, Robbie said, "The old man told me to let you choose your own last target if you would like."

"I do appreciate the offer," I replied, "but I prefer to just take it as it falls. However, I sure would like my last mission to be with a crew that has a lot of experience."

"I think I can handle that for you," Robbie said.

Knowing that I only had one more combat mission to fly before going home, I suddenly felt like an old man at twenty years of age.

The synthetic oil plant at Politz was mission thirty-five. Robbie sure kept his word, because I was assigned as the bombardier for a lead crew that was also making a thirty-fifth mission. Their regular bombardier was in the hospital, so I substituted for him. Forty-seven aircraft took off on the mission, but the intense and accurate flak at the target would shoot down eight aircraft and damage twenty-four. As the lead ship in the low box, we must have had an angel riding on our shoulders because, in spite of the heavy concentration of accurate flak in the target, we received no battle damage. We caused heavy destruction to the target. I just hope the price we paid – eighty men lost – made it worth the effort.

As we entered the traffic pattern for our landing, it suddenly dawned on me that Robbie had assigned me to this crew so I could share in their victory pass over the field and know it was also my victory pass. On the downwind leg the pilot got on the intercom and asked, "Is everyone ready for our victory pass?" We all answered with, "Roger." The flight engineer added, "Just don't try to roll this big ass bird, skipper!" I tightened up my seat belt and watched things rushing toward me. We were really on the deck when we crossed the touchdown end of the runway.

This crew would have a big party in the combat crew mess hall that night. They invited me to join them but I told them, "I really appreciate your offer, but it should be your crew's party and I would be an outsider."

After interrogation and gun cleaning, I headed for the O Club. I was very glad that I did, because my card-playing friends, my going-to-London friends, and others had a big surprise party planned for me. Beer flowed continuously and the bartender fixed me several of my favorite sandwiches—corn beef and cheese with hot English mustard on freshly baked bread (freshly stolen from the combat crew mess hall).

Robbie was in the club with Maj. Frank Richardson, our new squadron CO, and they came over to join the party. The major asked, "What are your plans, Bill?"

"My short-range plans are to go back to the States, away from war, and get some real rest. I have been offered a spot on a War Bond tour with some movie stars for a six-month assignment, but I understand that means a different city almost every day. It would probably be a fun assignment, but it really doesn't fit in with my career plans. My long-range plans are all pointed towards a military career in the Army Air Forces. So I do have to consider which assignments would be beneficial to my career."

"That's good, sound thinking," replied the major. "I wish you the best of luck."

The party broke up when the club closed. As he was leaving, Robbie said, "How about coming to the office for coffee in the morning?" I agreed and headed for my bed, looking forward to my first carefree night of sleep since I started combat flying.

CHAPTER 11

Second Combat Tour

Every soldier since Caesar's legions has known better than to volunteer for anything. Apparently, history was lost on me. Robbie wanted more than to just have a cup of coffee with me that morning. He really leaned on my sense of duty to convince me to volunteer for a second combat tour.

I remember well his opening statement, "You are one of only two radar bombardiers in our squadron and the only one in the whole group that is also a navigator." He then pointed out, "Your first combat tour was completed without being wounded and with only three crash landings. If you sign on for a second tour, you will be a tremendous help to the squadron and the group, and you will be appointed to the position of lead radar/bombardier for the squadron." He also said, "When I rotate back to the States I will recommend you for the squadron bombardier position. That would probably mean a promotion to captain, and I'm sure you can see how that would help your career in the Army Air Forces."

Since I had already made up my mind to remain in the service for a military career, I allowed ambition to cloud my logical thinking. I decided to forget about the six-month War Bond tour with movie stars. Agreement to start a second combat tour as the lead radar/bombardier for our squadron meant I also decided I would not be going home until the war in Europe was over.

The first mission on my second combat tour is still fresh in my mind—Hamburg, Germany! My crew for that day had completed ten combat missions. They had already checked out as a lead crew and we were assigned as deputy lead for the squadron. I felt embarrassed because of the look of respect on all of their faces when we introduced ourselves. They all knew I was on my second combat tour. I put a piece of gum in my mouth and tried to act nonchalant. However, as I chewed harder on my gum, I bit my tongue with enough force to produce blood in my mouth and tears in my eyes. The crew could see what had happened and, after a good laugh, we all headed for the aircraft.

The group put up thirty-seven aircraft that day. Major Richardson was flying group lead on the seven-hour trip into Germany. The mission started out like an easy one. From takeoff to the target area, everything was routine. No flak and no enemy fighters. Then, as we started the bomb run at 28,000 feet, all hell broke loose.

Flak was so thick it made the sky look black. From the IP (initial point), where we turned on to the bomb run, we were in the most intense flak I had seen on any of my combat missions. Because of the density of the flak and the way the bursts pushed us around the sky, it was difficult to keep the indices of the bombsight from coming together until we reached the AP (aiming point).

Although the bomb run took only one and a half minutes, it seemed much longer. We reached the AP and the indices on my bombsight came together, causing the bombs to drop one by one. Just as the last bomb left the bomb rack, I reached for my mike to give the pilot the same call that I had given to so many other pilots, "Bombs away, let's go home." All I got out of my mouth was, "Bombardier to pilot, bombs—." A direct hit tore away most of the nose of our aircraft. The last thing I recalled before I slipped entirely into blackness was watching in total fascination as a small piece of flak lazily ricocheted around what was left of the nose of our aircraft and I saw the navigator reach up with his gloved hand and catch that piece of flak. Everything seemed to move in slow motion, and I passed out in a few seconds.

The navigator, who miraculously was not injured, noticed that flak had severed my oxygen line. He started bringing me back to the world of reality with a walk-around oxygen bottle. When I regained my senses, I knew I was out of action for a time because I couldn't move my right leg and I had no feeling in either arm.

Although we were badly shot up, the pilot and co-pilot brought us back to Polebrook without further incident until they tried to lower the landing gear. Flak had severed a line and put our hydraulic system out of commission. The flight engineer called the pilot on the intercom and told him, "I cranked the gear down by hand but one tire had been destroyed by flak, so I cranked the gear back up." The pilot decided to make a wheels-up landing. A couple of the gunners carried me back into the radio room and braced me with parachutes for a rough landing. On the final leg of our landing pattern, the co-pilot fired a red flare to alert the medics. We made a wheels-up landing in the dirt off the right side of the runway. The medics were waiting for me when we stopped and they took me to the base hospital to clean me up. Within an hour of our landing, I was on my way back to the 303rd General Hospital.

Thus began my forty-five-day stay in the casualty ward of the hospital. During that time, the doctors dug the flak and most of the plexiglas out of my arms, sewed up the tendon in my right leg, and decided to leave the small, new-moon-shaped piece of flak in my right knee cap because, as the doctor said, "To remove it would have drained the water off my knee and left me with a stiff leg."

Two weeks after the medics finished cutting on me, Robbie

Flak

and Major Richardson came to visit me and presented me with a Distinguished Flying Cross. As Robbie pinned the DFC on my pajamas, it was obvious that he was really choked up for talking me into flying a second combat tour. It was difficult for him to read the citation, so I said to him, "Hey, Robbie, it was my decision to fly another combat tour. I'll be out of here in a couple of weeks."

The commanding officer of the hospital came into the room and pinned a Purple Heart Medal, for being wounded, on my pajamas, next to the DFC. He also told me that prior to discharging me from the hospital he would have special orders issued sending me to the flak home at Spetchley Park Manor, near Stratford-upon-Avon, for two weeks of R and R (rest and recuperation).

Major Richardson spoke up then. "Make it one week, Doc. I need him back in the squadron." Then he said, "I'll make it up to you, Bill, but we are getting in so many new crews I really need you back at the squadron so you and Robbie can help get them ready to fly combat missions." Before leaving, Major Richardson told me, "Your friend and mentor, Elzia Ledoux, was promoted to lieutenant colonel and left to go back to the States. However,

Distinguished Flying Cross

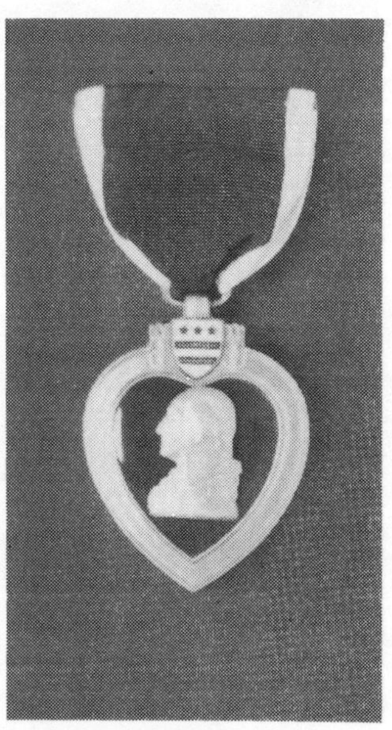

Purple Heart Medal

he learned of your being wounded and called me from London. He asked me to tell you he heard about your career decision. He said he wishes you a speedy recovery plus a long and satisfying Army Air Forces career. He also said he hopes you and he will have the opportunity to serve together again."

The day for my discharge from the hospital finally arrived. That forty-five days had seemed more like a year. As I was taking my hospital clearance papers through the necessary steps, a nurse handed me special orders for one week at the Spetchley Park flak home. Then she took them back as she said, "Lieutenant, let me check on these orders because combat-wounded patients are supposed to receive two weeks of R and R."

I told her, "Don't bother, nurse. My commanding officer misses me so much that he and the doctor decided my wounds only deserved one week of R and R." The poor nurse must not have realized I was joking because she was shaking her head and looking sad as I got on the bus.

In town I took the train to the city of Worchester. At Worchester I boarded a bus that took me to Spetchley Park. That gorgeous estate was set in a beautiful, tranquil English countryside. Many buildings, stables, and retainer quarters made up the manor, but the focal point was a stately early eighteenth-century manor house which contained many artifacts that probably dated back to the very early days of the manor. The lawn surrounding the main house looked like a putting green. The formal garden at the back of the estate which ended at a crystal clear lake made a spectacular setting. The very generous owners of the estate had made it available for 8th Air Force combat crews to get a little rest from the rigors of flying combat.

At the registration desk, I learned that the administration of the manor was under the auspices of the British Red Cross. There were three very attractive British Red Cross hostesses, and one of the girls, Joanna, told me, "There are only eleven combat crew members here at the present time so you will not be crowded." I must have appeared amazed to learn there were only eleven people in a place that could easily have handled 100 people in comfort. She explained, "Other titled British people have turned their manors over to the British Red Cross for the same purpose, so there really is no need for crowding."

Joanna called a footman and asked him to take me to find some country squire clothing and to get me settled in my room. It had been over two years since I had worn anything but a

Spetchley Park Manor (flak home).

uniform. After a shave and a bath, I put on the tweeds laid out for me. That heather aroma and soft comfort caused my whole body to completely relax. It seemed so strange that the locale, the friendliness of the people, and the wonderful soft tweeds could have such a soothing effect on my body and on my mind.

I returned to the first floor just in time for high tea. There were several other "guests of the manor" present, and we all got acquainted over tea, poured from a beautiful, ornate silver tea service. We also had little sandwiches served on small, matching silver plates. One of the guests, by the name of Ben, was from my bomb group but in a different squadron.

Joanna and a couple of the other hostesses joined our group, and Joanna handed me a carte blanche which listed all of the activities that were available for guests. Ben pointed out several activities that he found enjoyable, especially horseback riding. I told him, "I'm afraid that would be a little too strenuous for me in my present physical condition." I noticed that an evening at the Shakespeare Memorial Theater at Stratford-upon-Avon was on the list. Ben said he, too, would enjoy taking in a Shakespeare play.

When I asked Joanna how we could go to a play, she offered to take Ben and me the next evening. She left to make three reservations for us and, upon returning, said, "We are in luck because tomorrow is the last performance of *King Lear,* to be followed in two days by the opening of *Hamlet.* I made reservations for both plays, just in case the two of you would enjoy seeing them in the same week. Of course, the tickets are gifts to you from the British Red Cross."

Ben and I jumped at the opportunity. When I mentioned to Joanna that I studied both of those Shakespeare tragedies in school, she seemed surprised to hear a Yank who knew that there were both tragedies and comedies by Shakespeare.

We were told that dinner would be served at 8:00 P.M., by candlelight, and it would be formal, i.e., full uniform. When I went to my room, I found that my uniform had been very neatly pressed and my shoes shined. King George (that was his real name) knocked on my door to see if there was anything I needed. He was the one who got the very comfortable tweeds for me upon my arrival and informed me, "I shall have the honor of being your footman while you are a guest of the manor." When I learned that he was the one responsible for the pressing of my uniform and the shining of my shoes, I tried to express my appreciation but all he would say was, "I shall find it a pleasure to be of service to you, sir." Sure would be easy to get used to that type of living.

After a shower, I put on my uniform and went down to the dining room. Since Ben and I seemed to hit it off at the high tea, we were seated at the same table. Ben was a captain, a pilot and, like me, he had signed on for another combat tour. His combat crew had already departed for the States, so he would be flying as a lead pilot or an instructor pilot. Ben had been there for three days already, but he had a two-week stay. He could not believe it when I told him that my squadron CO would only OK a one-week stay for me. However, when he learned of my three ratings, he said, "You're lucky to get one week because all of the squadrons have a real critical shortage in your triple ratings." He added, "Every squadron has plenty of pilots, but you will probably be one of two or three radar-qualified bombardiers and navigators in the whole group." We discussed the possibility of the two of us flying on the same crew but soon decided that it was virtually impossible, since he was in the 511th Bomb Squadron and I was in the 509th.

After dinner, Ben invited me to go along on a bicycle tour the next morning with him and several other guests. I really needed some exercise, so we agreed to meet at breakfast.

What a wonderful night of restful sleep. At 7:00 A.M., King

George awakened me with a tall glass of cold fruit juice and my choice of coffee or tea. I chose the tea—after all, when in Rome do as the Romans do.

Ben and the other bicycling nuts had saved me a place at their table. Our breakfast consisted of more fruit juice, coffee or tea, ham, fresh eggs, English muffins with the ever present home-made jam, and a cold glass of fresh milk "for anyone who wanted one"—and we all wanted one!

One of the rules of the manor was that no one started eating until the table hostess was seated. That morning, Jan was our table hostess and she was quite late. She rushed in full of apologies and said, "No one knocked me up this morning." We were so stunned by her remark that no one even snickered. We later learned that in England, one says "knock me up" for "wake me up."

After breakfast, we checked out our bicycles and started our three-hour tour of the peaceful countryside. At one point we all got off our bicycles in a little town square just to smell the flowers that surrounded a fountain. During a short pause in the middle of a war, there I was, walking around smelling the flowers. It just seemed to be the natural thing to do at the time and it gave me such a feeling of peace.

We arrived back at the manor just in time for lunch. Joanna was our table hostess and she told Ben and me, "We should be ready to leave for Stratford-upon-Avon by three, so we will have time to see some of the town and have dinner before the play."

Returning to my room to take a bath and prepare for the evening, I found that King George again had a uniform pressed and laid out on my bed. Just after I entered my room, he knocked on the door to see if I needed anything. I told him, "No, but I appreciate your asking."

He did not leave right away, so I sensed that he wanted to ask me something. He finally said, "Would it be too much of an imposition, sir, to ask if you will bring me a program for the play?" I assured him that I would certainly bring him a program.

I shaved, took a nice hot bath, and got into my neatly pressed uniform. Joanna, Ben and I had a "spot of tea" and then departed for Stratford in Joanna's beautiful Bentley. It was only a fifteen- or twenty-mile trip, and we arrived in plenty of time to act like tourists. Joanna mentioned that as long as she had lived in the area, she had never taken the scenic boat trip on the Avon River. Ben and I treated her to the boat trip and to dinner in the theater restaurant prior to the play.

Entering the theater, I remembered to pick up an extra program for King George. The play was a very meaningful experience for me and I lived every scene, since I had studied it in school. We had tea and crumpets in the theater restaurant after the play and everyone in the audience and the cast must have decided to do the same thing because the place was packed. Joanna knew several of the actors, who came to our table to greet her. She introduced us to her friends and told them we were guests of the manor. It was quite a thrill for Ben and me to meet some real Shakespearean actors.

Our trip back to the manor took about two hours because of the necessity of driving slowly due to blackout rules. On the way, we heard a noise in the air and Joanna told us, "That is probably a buzz bomb heading for London."

It was after midnight when we got back to the manor. When I climbed the stairs to my room, I could see King George seated in a chair at the end of the hall. When I reached him, he was asleep. I touched him on the shoulder and he jumped up and said, "I'm sorry I allowed myself to go to sleep, sir."

"It is after midnight, and most people are asleep by this time," I replied. "Here is your program for that wonderful Shakespeare play." I invited him to come by early in the morning so that I could tell him about the play.

At 6:00 A.M., King George knocked on my door, carrying a tray with a complete breakfast. When I asked him how he managed a complete breakfast so early in the morning, he smiled (for the first time) and said, "Knowing people in the right places." I invited him to sit down while I ate the breakfast, so we could talk about the play. He told me that he had read all of the Shakespeare plays, but had never seen one on the stage. We discussed many other things, and I learned that he and his wife were raising two grandchildren. Their only son had been in the RAF and was killed during the early days of the Battle of Britain. The children's mother was killed in a German bombing raid on Coventry while the two children were on a school field trip. King George's wife, a schoolteacher, had also read all of the Shakespeare plays. I learned that he was fifty-two years old and had served in the British Army in North Africa, where he lost a leg. That last bit of information was a complete surprise to me because he did not use a cane or walk with a limp.

When I had finished my breakfast, King George took away the tray. I got dressed for an early morning golf game with Ben and two others with whom we went on the bicycle tour. The other three enjoyed playing golf with me because my high score made them look good. The last time on a golf course for me had been before I enlisted; but then, that just sounded like an excuse.

That night, after another memorable candlelight dinner, a group of RAF combat crew members from a nearby RAF base came to the manor to pay us a visit. We shared combat stories and really enjoyed the time spent together. I played five games of darts with several of them and actually won one game. Our genial hostesses served everyone tea and tarts, and whiskey and beer were available on request. After inviting us to visit their base, the RAF guys left and we turned in for another restful night of sleep.

The next morning at breakfast, Ben and I decided to just relax and play some gin rummy since we would be going to another play that evening. Two of the hostesses came over to our card table later in the morning and we played several hands of bridge until lunchtime. Lunch was an informal picnic on the rolling grassy lawn by the lake. We all agreed it would really be difficult to go back to flying combat and eating GI food after the type of life we had enjoyed at the manor.

Ben and I joined Joanna for the trip to Stratford in her auto. When we went by the kiosk to pick up our tickets for the performance that evening, I asked the clerk if it was possible to purchase tickets for a future play without specifying a play or date. When I learned that it was possible, I bought four tickets to give to King George before I had to leave the manor in a couple of days.

Hamlet was just as enjoyable as *King Lear.* We stopped in the theater restaurant for tea and crumpets before starting our slow trip back to the manor. Again, King George was waiting for me, and I gave him the program for *Hamlet.* He told me how much he and his wife enjoyed reading the program on *King Lear.* We bade each other good night and I hit the sack.

At breakfast Ben invited me to go fishing with several others. One of the hostesses learned what we planned to do and had a picnic lunch prepared for us to take along. We all caught as many fish as we could carry. That night the chef prepared a fish dinner for everyone, the likes of which I had never before tasted.

The days went by so quickly, and now it was time for me to leave and go back to flying combat. When King George awakened me with cold juice and a pot of tea, I asked him to step inside for a minute. I gave him the four tickets for the Shake-

"At ease" at Spetchley Park Manor.

speare Theater and told him, "This is just a small token of my appreciation for all that you've done for me during my stay at the manor. I hope you, your wife, and your grandchildren will enjoy the play." King George really got choked up, taking my hand in both of his, and thanked me most sincerely. He then told me that he and his wife would pray for my safe return to my family in America.

After breakfast, I started saying thank you and goodbye to all of the wonderful staff at the manor. Ben said he would look me up when he got back to the base. King George brought down my bags that he had so thoughtfully packed while I was having breakfast.

Perhaps it sounds corny, but, as I was leaving, I remembered a line from Shakespeare: "Parting is such sweet sorrow."

CHAPTER 12

"Breakfast at three, briefing at four!"

As I lay there in my bunk, waiting for the squadron clerk's call, I found myself staring at my watch. The circular motion of the luminous sweep second hand reminded me of the hunk of flak that ricocheted around the shattered nose of our aircraft just two short months ago—and the apprehension mounted.

"All right you guys, hit the deck. Breakfast at three, briefing at four!" yelled the clerk in a voice that sounded like a buzz bomb. At least now maybe my apprehension would ease up because there was always a lot of work for me to do between briefing and takeoff time. I had to get the guns loaded in the chin turret of our new B-17G, check the arming wires and safety pins in the bombs, and make a last-minute review of the target photos.

I always filled my flak helmet with water the night before and left it on the pot belly stove near my bunk so I could have a hot water shave before breakfast. My shave took three minutes and my cold water shower in the little house out back took even less time.

Breakfast in the combat crew mess hall was the typical breakfast-before-a-mission type: hot cakes and syrup, one fresh egg on top, a glass of real milk, and the ever-present sulphur pills. That type of breakfast must have been considered a fringe benefit for flying combat; on the days we didn't fly, we had either powdered eggs or S-O-S with biscuits and powdered milk. When we wrote home about it we referred to S-O-S as "same old stuff," but among the troops it was well known as "same old shit."

As I sat in the briefing room, waiting to learn the target for the day, I found myself studying the faces of the crew I would be flying with. At least they weren't a new crew; they had already completed twenty-five missions. Their regular bombardier was grounded that day because of a head cold. I had known their co-pilot, Pete, for some time as we went to London on a three-day pass and we often played bridge together. Although they were telling jokes and lying about their dates over the weekend, I sensed a tenseness about the crew – or did I see my own tenseness mirrored in their faces? Was I getting gun-shy just because I had been hit and spilled a little blood on my last mission? I put that thought out of my mind immediately and joined in the joking and lying. After all, I had decided, back in Sioux City, that I would be indestructible in combat.

"Attention!" Everyone popped to and could hear the proverbial pin drop as the group commander, Colonel Burns, and his staff strode up to the front of the briefing room. The operations officer told us to be seated as he pulled the cover off the map. The usual *"oohs"* and *"aahs"* filled the room. It had always seemed strange to me that, no matter what the target – Berlin, Munich, Leipzig, or a milk run – when the cover was pulled off the map everyone said either *"ooh"* or *"aah,"* myself included. A head shrinker would probably be able to make something out of whether a guy said *"ooh"* or *"aah."*

As the briefing progressed, we found that we had something special on tap. Our normal targets were strategic areas, including marshaling yards, oil fields, ball-bearing plants, and air fields, and we would hit them from 26,000 to 28,000 feet. That day we were going to join the "Battle of the Bulge." The battle in Belgium had been going on for some time now, but practically all the aircraft in Europe had been grounded for over a week due to miserable weather. This day, just four days before Christmas, we were going to bomb from 15,000 feet and just over the front lines. That meant a special briefing and target study for the bombardiers after the general briefing.

The rest of the crew was already in the aircraft when I climbed aboard, just as the sun made a valiant effort to burn through the ever-present British fog. Our takeoff time was two hours later than usual because of the special bombardier briefing, and I discovered that the gunners had already fitted the guns into the chin turret for me. That's a job that is next to impossible to do while wearing gloves. In cold weather, without gloves, if you touched the cold metal your skin froze to it. After flying thirty-six combat missions, I was working on about the fourth layer of skin on my hands. I expressed my appreciation to the gunners and promised to buy them a beer at the Rose and Crown pub in Oundle when we got back.

After checking over the twelve 500-pound bombs in the bomb bay that we were going to deliver to Hitler's elite, I climbed up to my office in the nose. It seemed that I just got seated and strapped in when the green flare was fired and we taxied out to the end of the runway.

Our takeoff was smooth and we joined up with the rest of the squadron formation over King's Cliff. We were flying deputy lead for the squadron, and our squadron was assigned to the high box in the group formation.

As we headed out over the channel in a good, tight formation, I decided to experiment with the special map of our target area that was given to us at the special bombardier briefing. The intelligence officer said that in the event we were about to be captured, we should eat the map because it was made out of a special paper that was easily digestible. I bit off a small corner to test it, and after a considerable amount of chewing, I managed to swallow the cud. I hoped that nothing caused me to have to eat that 36 x 24-inch map.

Over the intercom we heard, "Pilot to crew, we are now at oxygen altitude. Bombardier, you run the oxygen checks today at ten-minute intervals." My reply was a rather guttural, "Roger," because that damn map might have been digestible but it sure took a long time to get into the system. The navigator advised the crew that we were entering the area where we could expect enemy fighters. We had all test-fired our guns over the English Channel, and now the gunners began scanning their individual sectors of the sky.

Nearing the point where we would start our bomb run, I found that all my apprehension had left me and my training took over. The bombsight was all set up for the bomb run, and I used the last few minutes to go over the map of the target area and assure myself that I had located my exact aiming point. The navigator told me that we were two minutes from the IP (initial point). I have always been amazed that when we reached the IP and started the bomb run, I was able to actually fly a big, lumbering bomber through the use of the two correction knobs the size of silver dollars on the right side of my bombsight.

Now it was time for me to go to work. As we turned onto the bomb run, the pilot flipped on the PPI (planned position indicator), which transferred control of the aircraft to my bombsight. A quick check of the bomb panel revealed that everything was ready, and I flipped the toggle switch that opened the gaping bomb bay doors. Our aircraft was being bounced around like a cork in a heavy sea due to the intensely heavy antiaircraft fire. I raised up from the bombsight to make a last-minute check of the bombing panel and I noticed that the sky was white with flak. *White!* I had never seen white flak before. Our normal flak opposition from the German 88 filled the sky with flak that was as black as coal or sometimes red, when they tried to vector their fighters into specific areas. The white flak aroused my curiosity, but it would be many months before I learned that it came from our own antiaircraft weapons shooting at us. The MPI (main point of impact) for our bombs was exactly as briefed, but after we took off on the mission the ground troops advanced into that area and our bombs fell on them. Due to the heavy clouds, miserable weather, and general lack of communication between ground and air, our ground troops must have thought they were being bombed by the Germans. They opened up with 155mm howitzers.

With our salvo bomb drop, all twelve 500-pound bombs would leave the bomb bay at once. The indices of the bombsight came together, and the bombs all left their shackles. As all of those bombs dropped at once, our aircraft lurched upward like the motion of a kite in a March wind and then resumed normal flight. There sure wasn't any need to call "Bombs away" over the intercom, but I did so out of habit. After the radio operator checked the bomb bay for me, I flipped the toggle switch to clear the bomb rack and then closed the bomb bay doors.

After putting the cover on the bombsight, I pulled the control box and gunsight for the chin turret over in front of me and began watching for enemy fighters. All at once there was a blinding flash, and I was slammed back against the firewall as the aircraft did a wingover and went into an uncontrolled, inverted dive. There was a terrific pain in my head and I felt myself getting numb all over as darkness surrounded me and I began to slip into unconsciousness. I wondered if I was passing out, as I had done on my last mission, or if I was actually dying.

When I regained consciousness, Joe, the navigator, was standing over me, trying to clean my face. The aircraft was again in level flight but we had lost a lot of altitude before the pilots pulled us out of that dive. We were still losing altitude. As I looked around the nose of the aircraft, or what was left of the nose, it looked like the inside of a discarded catsup bottle. Blood was everywhere—my blood. I discovered that we took a direct hit in the number-three engine, knocking it completely out of the wing. A piece of the flak had penetrated my flak helmet and lodged in the center of my forehead. The rapid descent of our dive must have acted as a pump attached to the hole in my head to pump out my blood. I didn't feel any pain—just numbness. But all of my limbs moved.

I looked around to see what other damage we had. The hole left by the number-three engine was a ball of fire, and the wing was starting to burn. All of the plexiglas in the nose was gone; only the aluminum framing remained, and the wind rushing into the nose had the navigator and me pushed up against the fire wall. Any movement we made felt like swimming in thick molasses. The pilot was yelling over the intercom at the navigator, wanting to know if we were OK because he could see the nose was almost completely shot away. I nodded and Joe reported that we were all right. The pilot told me to open the bomb bay doors, and then he pushed the bailout alarm. Joe and I got out of our flak suits, preparing for our bailout. Joe then jumped out the front escape hatch.

As I opened the bomb bay doors, I glanced at the altimeter on the bomb panel and saw that we were at just over 2,300 feet, which meant we had lost almost 13,000 feet while the pilot and co-pilot struggled to bring us out of our inverted dive. I started to follow the navigator out the front escape hatch but the pilot, not knowing that I had been wounded, called me on the intercom and said, "Bill, I can't get an answer from the tail gunner on the intercom and all the other gunners have bailed out. How about checking on him for me?"

"Roger," I replied. I unhooked one of the "D" rings of my chest pack parachute, tucked the chute under my left arm, and inched my way back through the bomb bay into the radio room, then into the waist section. I saw that we had much more damage than just the nose and engine. One of the waist gunners was very obviously dead, so I passed him and crawled back into the tail section. I could see the tail gunner but did not know, until I reached him, that most of his head was gone. I worked my way back through the waist section, the radio room, the bomb bay, and up to the cockpit. When I stood up to tell the pilot what I had found, there was no one in the cockpit. I was alone in a burning aircraft that was now losing altitude more rapidly.

I groped my way back to the bomb bay as I rehooked the "D" ring on my parachute harness and dove out head-first. Many thoughts passed through my mind as I dove out those bomb bay doors: *I'll never volunteer again . . . The escape and evasion officer said don't open your chute right away because the enemy ground troops will open fire at you . . . 2,300 feet on the altimeter before I went back to the tail section and the aircraft was in a shallow dive . . .* That last thought made up my mind. I pulled the rip cord.

I must have been falling flat because when the chute opened, I was swung upward like a pendulum. On my downward swing my feet hit the ground. God only knows how low I was when I pulled that rip cord.

On the ground, I clawed out of my parachute harness and stood up. I was elated just to be able to stand up and walk. The snow was very deep and made walking difficult, but it no doubt saved me from having two broken legs, to say the least.

After looking around a few minutes, I found Pete, the co-pilot. I cannot express the relief I felt to find that I was not alone in enemy territory. I learned from Pete that the pilot and ball turret gunner had been killed by small-arms fire while they were coming down in their chutes and that he had not been able to find any of the others. I told him about finding two of the gunners dead at their positions before I left the aircraft. Pete noticed my bloody face for the first time and asked me if I could walk. I put my hand to my forehead and, in spite of all the blood on my face, I could feel the metal still stuck in the center of my forehead. That was a frightening feeling. However, the wound seemed to be well clotted so I assured Pete I was all right. He helped me clean the blood from my face with snow.

We knew that we were close to the front lines when our aircraft was hit, so we decided to start walking and try to meet up with some American ground troops. Because of the heavy snow that was still coming down, I was not able to get a fix on the direction we were heading. After we walked for an hour or so, we rounded a clump of trees and walked into a German encampment. The Germans were just as surprised as we were. Their rifles looked as big as antitank guns pointing at us, and all we could do was put up our hands.

Standing there, surrounded by Germans, with our hands in the air, I wondered if we would have any chance to escape before they sent us to one of their prisoner-of-war camps in Germany. One thing was sure: Our war appeared to be over.

CHAPTER 13

Prisoner of War

Pete and I were placed in a corral made out of coiled barbed wire with very sharp points that the Germans hastily built as we were brought into the camp. There was nothing in the containment area, so we both sat on the ground and waited. The Germans had taken all of our heavy leather, fur-lined flying clothes after putting us in the corral, so sitting on the ground was a very cold experience.

A German medic came into the corral to check on my head wound. After washing the blood off my face, he found the hunk of flak sticking out of the center of my forehead. He felt it and tried to pull it out. I told him, "That hurts like hell," and I motioned for him to leave it alone. The guy actually had a look of concern on his face as he dusted the wound with some kind of powder and wrapped a rag around my forehead. That was the total medical treatment I received from the Germans during my captivity.

When the medic left, Pete and I began to plan how we would escape and make our way to our own lines. We decided we would have a better chance after dark, when the Germans were asleep, because there appeared to be over 200 soldiers in the camp.

It became very dark as the campfires burned lower and the Germans turned in for the night. The guard at our corral sat down and leaned against a tree, with his bayonet-equipped rifle on the ground next to him. He soon began to snore, so Pete and I waited for the right opportunity to escape. Everything was very quiet in the camp, and a couple of hours had passed since the guard started to snore, so we decided to make our break.

Pete was a big Texan and he told me, "I'll hold up the barbed wire so you can crawl under it and get a pole to hold the wire up for me." As I was crawling under the coiled wire, it slipped out of Pete's hands and dug into my back, making it impossible for me to move. The noise awakened the guard; he grabbed his rifle and came running toward us, shouting at us to *"halte."* Pete raised his hands above his head and the guard motioned for me to stand up. I kept pointing to the barbed wire which was imbedded in my back, but I didn't move fast enough for the guard. He jabbed me in the rear with his bayonet. I yelled "Damn!" as I pushed my way through the barbed wire and stood up.

When I yelled, Pete went after the guard, but the guard just placed his rifle in Pete's face and fired, killing him on the spot. My hands were in the air but I was stalking slowly toward that guard so I could get a real good look at that bastard. I wanted to remember his face in case I ever got out of this situation and had an opportunity to avenge Pete's unnecessary killing.

By that time, the entire camp was awake. I was quickly surrounded by a bunch of German soldiers, who blindfolded me and tied my hands behind my back with heavy rope. I remained in that condition the entire length of my captivity, except for short periods twice a day when my hands were untied so that I could relieve myself. The blindfold, however, remained on.

I was taken to a cave and put inside. A German, who spoke to me in English with a British accent, said, "If you remove the blindfold, untie your hands, move the tarp at the cave entrance, or try to escape you will be shot without warning." He also told me, "The guard who prevented your escape will be on duty at the cave entrance every night." Before leaving he took my dog tags, watch, and my silver crash bracelet. He also found my escape kit, which contained gold coins, silk maps, and a German phrase book, in the right leg pocket of my summer flying suit. So, he took my summer flying suit. I was then left with only my robin's egg blue heated suit, designed to plug into the electrical system of the aircraft, and the winter and summer underwear beneath the heated suit. The German departed, leaving me with my anger and disbelief, as I remembered Pete's being shot and dragged off by his feet just before I was blindfolded.

Since I last ate at 0300 hours, before taking off on my last combat mission, it had been well over twenty-four hours since I had had any food. Gnawing hunger pangs began.

I lay down on my side, on the cold dirt floor of the cave, and fell asleep due to sheer exhaustion. I had no idea how long I had been asleep when I was awakened by someone who brought me a hot bowl of rotten-smelling turnip soup and a piece of stale black bread that had a sour smell. As I was fed the soup and bread, no words were spoken, and then the person left the cave. Only a few minutes passed when someone came back and fed me some raw turnips and water. When I bit into the last turnip I felt something crawling around in my mouth, and I spat out the whole mess. It seemed like at least a day before I was fed more foul-smelling turnip soup, sour black bread, and rancid water. The guards were now removing the ropes from my wrists long enough for me to feed and relieve myself, but the blindfold still remained. After a short period of time, more black bread and water. This same procedure went on for what must have been several days before my interrogation began.

It became rather obvious that an attempt was being made to break down my mental processes by first making me lose track of time. It worked well, because being blindfolded and being fed on an irregular schedule made me lose all ability to keep up with the time. All I could do was wait to see what would happen next.

Two men came into the cave, laughing and joking with each other. They took me by my arms and led me to the interrogation room. I was placed on a stool, still blindfolded and with my hands tied behind my back. A man in front of me again warned, "If you try to remove your blindfold or ropes you will be shot without warning." He was speaking English with a British accent, and I felt he was probably the same one who gave me the warning the first night in the cave.

He began the questioning in a friendly tone of voice. I answered his first question with: "William L. Cramer, Jr., Lieutenant, O-2033061." I began to detect anger in his voice because I answered with name, rank, and serial number to every one of his questions. Finally, I was taken back to the cave and pushed roughly inside.

The rotten raw turnips, the horrible turnip soup, the stale black bread, and the water with the stagnant smell and taste resumed at irregular periods. At that point, I had completely lost track of time and I wondered if their interrogation techniques would cause me to lose my mind – or worse, to lose my will to resist. Lying on that cold dirt floor was beginning to make every bone in my body ache continuously. Sleeping on the hard ground, with my hands tied behind my back, was becoming more and more difficult. At times, my arms felt as if they would surely fall off. The irregular periods between receiving food and water became longer and longer.

Each time I was taken back to the cave I tried to move to a different part so I could become familiar with the whole place. In some areas there was a rancid or cheese odor, and I began to speculate that this was probably a farmer's storage cave for his cheese. I was forcing myself to speculate on everything about that cave so that my mind would keep working on something.

After what must have been several days, I was again taken to the interrogation room with a man on each arm. The same German began to work on me once more. He started out by ruffling some papers and informing me, "I have here a complete dossier on you. I know all about your training and the type aircraft you were shot down in with your crew." I thought he was just feeding me a bunch of bull until he told me my aircraft had a big triangle J on the tail. That really shook me until I forced my thoughts back to reality and reasoned that they probably just went out to the crash site and got the tail marking.

He again became very friendly and asked me about the type of navigation we used on the mission. When I repeated my name, rank, and serial number, my head suddenly seemed to explode. A hard, open-handed slap had been simultaneously applied to both of my ears. Next he asked about our bombing techniques. Name, rank, and serial number. Again, very hard simultaneous slaps to both ears.

The ear slaps continued for a very long period of time, even when no questions were being asked. The room had become very quiet. I knew someone was standing directly behind me because I could feel him breathing on the back of my neck and I smelled his nauseous garlic breath. Even with the pain in my arms and the terrible ringing noise in my ears, I must have still been thinking clearly because I realized they were just trying to let fear build up in me and make me wonder when the ear slaps would come again. Their technique was very effective, because those ear slaps were very painful outside as well as inside my head and I began to worry about permanent damage to my hearing.

The room remained very quiet as two men lifted me off the stool, carried me back to the cave, and threw me inside. Those same interrogation techniques continued on a daily basis for what must have been a couple of months.

Once again I was taken into the interrogation room. The interrogator got very confidential with me and told me, "I am a captain in the German Army and I assure you that I am not SS or Gestapo." He told me his name was Kurt, but I do not remember his last name. Kurt told me, "My job is to learn from you everything about your bombing and navigation techniques, with emphasis on the box." I was sure he was talking about the "black box" we used for radar navigation and radar bombing and which was then classified secret. He finally said, "Look, Lieutenant, you have held out much longer than I expected you would and I respect you for that. Why not spare yourself further pain and tell me what I need to know? You will then be sent to a prisoner-of-war camp in Germany, where you will receive humane treatment. After we win the war you will be sent back safely to your home in America."

He continued. "I must have the information because the German Air Force intelligence people are on their way and I want to get the information first." He asked me to explain "the box" to him. I barely got out my name, rank, and serial number before the chair was kicked out from under me. I fell heavily to the floor on my right shoulder. With my hands tied behind my back, the pain was excruciating enough to cause me to black out. It would have been so easy to just pass out, but I fought to maintain a state of awareness.

After they placed me back on the stool, he next asked me about navigation. Name, rank, serial number – and this time it was a rifle butt to the midsection. The feeling of helplessness I had from being beat up while blindfolded and not being able to see it coming was incredible to experience. I decided to forget about name, rank, and serial number and just remain silent.

He asked me three more questions and I did not answer. The room got very quiet, but I could hear the whispering of three very low voices – then nothing. After a very long period of silence, I was lifted off the stool and taken back to the cave.

For what must have been several days, I was given water but no food and was permitted to relieve myself twice a day. I was becoming very concerned about my weight loss due to no food for lengthy periods of time. I could feel that my ribs had no meat on them, and when I put my thumb and index finger around my wrist it was a very loose fit. Finally, two men came into the cave, took me by the arms, and led me to the interrogation room.

The first question out of Kurt's mouth was about our special bombing techniques. I just sat there and waited for his next move. I had heard the expression, "the silence is deafening," and it certainly described that silence. I resolved not to break the silence. I wondered if Kurt would.

Suddenly, someone grabbed both of my arms while another person forced open my mouth, reached in with a pair of pliers that tasted rusty, and pulled out one of my lower teeth. My mouth filled with blood. I was taken back to the entrance of the cave and tossed inside.

As I lay on the floor of the cave, shaking with pain and anger, I vowed to escape—somehow!

Again, several days passed with no food. Then I was awakened from a deep sleep of exhaustion and taken back to the room for more interrogation. I was seated on the stool and nothing was said. Finally, Kurt asked, "Lieutenant, are you now ready for a nice gentlemanly talk?"

I stood up, and in the loudest voice I could muster with a very sore mouth, I told him, "Captain, you can go to hell!"

Again I was grabbed from both sides and pushed back down on the stool while my mouth was forced open and the rusty pliers pulled out a tooth from the other side of my mouth. After being taken back to the cave and tossed inside, I was in such a rage that I hardly felt the pain of the last extraction.

As I lay on the cold floor of the cave, I knew that I must escape soon or that mad man would surely kill me trying to learn our techniques.

CHAPTER 14

The Escape

My mouth finally stopped bleeding. I was making a determined effort to control my anger and to bring my mind back to reality. I knew I must think rationally so that I would be able to make my escape and I knew it must be tonight.

It was strange how acute my sense of hearing had become until the two-handed ear slaps began. My sense of smell had also increased. Being blindfolded the past few months had apparently caused my other senses to take over to make up for my inability to see. It had been several days since the repeated ear slaps stopped, and my hearing seemed to be developing again. Movements outside the cave and beyond the entrance were becoming clearer to my ears.

The outside noises had decreased considerably, which indicated that the soldiers were getting ready to go to bed. I struggled to my feet and backed up to the wall of the cave. Moving my bound hands slowly along the wall, I searched for a sharp rock or something to use to saw through the ropes. My search was finally successful—a crack in the wall that had sharp edges became my tool. Sawing on the ropes took a long time, and I cut up my wrists so much they began to bleed. Finally, the ropes pulled apart. With my hands free, I yanked off the blindfold but could not see a thing. Everything was completely black. Was it possible that the ear slaps and the blindfold had caused me to go blind?

Praying that it was only a temporary loss, I groped along the wall until my hands touched the tarp at the entrance of the cave. I listened intently and then carefully pulled the tarp aside just slightly. Being careful not to make any noise, I stuck my head around the corner of the entrance. A cold wind hit my face, but with my eyes wide open I saw nothing but blackness. There certainly was no way I could escape without being able to see, so I lay on the floor and waited.

Utter fatigue must have caused me to drop off to sleep because the sound of someone snoring awakened me. My concerted effort to force myself to think clearly helped me to realize that it must be the guard outside the cave entrance. Pulling the tarp aside slightly, I could barely distinguish shapes and what appeared to be the flickering flames of bonfires. It was very difficult to keep myself from rubbing my eyes, but that probably would have delayed the return of my normal vision. Just closing my eyes for a while seemed to help. When I opened them again, the shapes became a little more clear. It was soon possible for me to discern the figure of the guard lying on the ground next to the entrance of the cave, with his rifle and helmet next to him.

After resting my eyes a little longer and praying the guard would not awaken, it was time to make my break. Leaving the cave and crawling on my belly, up to the side of the still snoring guard, my hands touched his rifle and a chill went up my spine. When I stood up with his rifle in my hands, I was staring down into the face of the guard who so needlessly had killed Pete. I brought the butt of the rifle down on his head three times with all the strength that I could muster. He did not make a sound. I removed his shoes, took his rifle and his helmet, and carefully made my way to what, hopefully, would be the outer perimeter of the camp. My movements were very slow and deliberate because I didn't want to step on a sleeping German. That would surely have been the end of my escape and my life.

I finally reached a dirt road which, God willing, would take me away from the German camp. My breathing was very labored due to the excitement of what I was doing. I sat down on the ground to put on the shoes I had taken from the dead guard. The Germans had taken my combat boots along with my flying clothes, and the only things between my feet and the frozen ground had been two pair of socks and my woolen fabric heated inserts that were plugged into my heated suit. What a sight I must have been—walking down a dirt road in Belgium in my baby blue heated suit with the cord (used to connect it to the aircraft electrical system) dangling along on the ground, carrying the German guard's rifle in one hand, his helmet in the other hand, and wearing his shoes.

After walking along that dirt road for a considerable period of time, a faint fringe of the sun arose in the sky behind me. I knew then that I was walking in a westerly direction. It seemed so strange to hear the peaceful singing of the morning birds while my heart beat so loudly out of excitement or fear.

All of a sudden, there was a noise in the gully beside the road. I dropped the helmet and brought the rifle up to fire. The noise of a rifle shot would not be very smart, but I knew that I would not allow myself to be recaptured under any circumstances. If I was to die, some Germans would have to join me.

A young voice was repeating, *"Mon ami, mon ami."* Although one year of French in high school did not make me fluent in French, I knew enough to understand that meant "my friend," so I decided to take a chance and lowered the rifle. A young boy, probably around ten or twelve years old, came out of the gully, held out his hand, and told me, *"Je m'appelle Claude."* We sat at the side of the road until I could stop my trembling from our encounter.

I learned that he was with a group from the Belgium underground who had seen us bail out of our burning aircraft almost three months before. That was my first realization that I had been a prisoner of war under almost continuous questioning for nearly three months. It had seemed to me like a year. My new friend told me he would take me to a Belgium safe house so I could get a bath and rest for a while. My smell must have been terrible, because he emphasized the bath.

We had a very slow walk through wooded areas for over two hours. Claude kept asking me if I was able to walk without pain. I replied each time, *"Oui, mon ami."*

I learned from Claude that I had been shot down near the town of Saint Hubert, northwest of Bastogne. German army units had been back and forth through the area and there were still many Gestapo and SS troops throughout Belgium looking for downed airmen and their underground helpers. According to Claude, this was the most dangerous period for the underground since the start of the German occupation of Belgium.

After dawn broke, we arrived at a farm. Claude introduced me to Mademoiselle Marie, the only name I was given. I learned later from Claude that Marie was the only one left of her family. Both of her parents and her two brothers were killed by the Germans in the early days of the occupation. Marie, in her mid to late twenties, spoke no English and I spoke very little French, so Claude, with a mixture of French and Pidgin English, was the interpreter.

My first meal in over two months consisted of eggs, cheese, a steak, white bread with freshly churned butter, lots of cold milk, and coffee. Just the smell of that food caused saliva to form at both corners of my mouth. Eating everything put in front of me, I soon had to stop because of a strange, rumbling sensation in the pit of my stomach which made me feel as though I might throw up everything. Claude and Marie filled a tub with hot water for me and found some civilian clothes that would allow me to blend in with others in the area. After I climbed into that wonderful tub of hot, sudsy water, Claude came in with a razor, brush, and soap and gave me a shave while I just relaxed and soaked out the filth and pain of the last three months.

While he was shaving me, I asked Claude to leave the mustache so that I could grow it like a curled RAF-type of mustache. That was the first shave I had had since the day I took off on my last mission.

When the bath was finished, I put on the clothes that Claude had brought in for me and exhaustion suddenly took over my body. I felt as though someone had turned on a tap and drained my body of all energy. Marie showed me to a room in the attic that had a downy soft bed, and I lay on the bed fully clothed. Marie was worried about my head wound. She was able to feel the piece of flak that was still imbedded in the front part of my skull, and it still hurt when touched. She applied some medicated salve, wrapped the wound with a sterile bandage, and then pulled the cotton soft comforter up to my chin and left.

Sleep came over me so fast that I did not even hear Marie close the door. The rest lasted for an unbelievable fourteen hours. In my dreams I relived my period as a prisoner of war. When I awoke, remembering how much pleasure I had received from bringing the rifle butt down on that German guard's head really began to bother me. It was not the killing itself, but the fact that I derived so much pleasure from killing the guard who had killed Pete.

Getting off the bed, I noticed a large basin and pitcher of water on the table next to the bed. I splashed cold water on my face. Claude and Marie heard me moving around and they both came up to the attic to see if I was all right. We all had a laugh about my sleeping fourteen hours. Marie told me she had prepared a late meal for all of us, and she left to finish putting it on the table. Claude said he had arranged to get me some identification papers in the morning at the next safe house, if I was rested enough to travel.

Marie's meal consisted of a delicious roast beef (baked with potatoes, carrots, and onions), a salad, freshly baked bread, and a homemade pie. I tried to explain to her that my grandmother fixed that very same meal every Sunday when the whole family congregated at her house. I told Marie the aromas that arose to the attic reminded me so much of home. Marie apparently had previously experienced other people who had gone for long periods without eating. She told me that I was welcome to all of the food I wanted but that I must be careful not to overload my stomach too soon.

After a wonderful meal, Claude informed me that we must leave for a new safe house very early in the morning. With his help, I tried to express my gratitude to Marie. She smiled and let me know that she understood what I was trying to say to her. However, what could one say to a person who was knowingly placing her own life in great danger to help you escape? I gave my full name and address to Marie and asked her to let me hear from her after the war. She promised to do that. Unfortunately, Marie, like my other helpers, might not have survived the war because I have never heard from her.

The next leg of my journey to freedom was a long trip in a produce truck with Claude to another farm. There, fake German identification papers were made up in my name with my photo attached. The farmer's wife laid out a big meal for us, and again, I tried to eat too much and had to run outside to lose everything in my stomach. The retching caused a very sore throat, and the only thing I could swallow was some warm milk that Claude heated for me on the stove.

My two new helpers were an elderly couple identified to me by Claude as longtime members of the FFI (French underground). It was difficult for me to say thank you and then goodbye to Claude, but I gave him my full name and home address, saying to him, "Please write to me after the war is over." He said that he would. Then he told me that I must leave quickly with my new helpers.

The three of us started walking to a small, nearby town where we were to board a train for Lille. My helpers both spoke English fairly well. They explained to me, "German soldiers will probably ask you for identity papers several times before we reach Lille. Don't worry, just show them your papers because they are very well done." I was never told the names of my new helpers, so I referred to them as Madame and Monsieur during our very long trip. The train was loaded with German soldiers and they checked identity papers every time we pulled out of a station. My helpers and I spent most of our time in a baggage car because the soldiers did not seem to be interested in that car. Our food consisted of French bread, cheese, and wine that either Madame or Monsieur obtained whenever we stopped at a station. It wasn't exactly a feast, but it kept us going.

One evening I asked Monsieur, "Why do you and your wife risk your lives to help me?"

"Je n'en sais pas," he said, "it just seems like the right thing to do." His mixing of French and English was helping me to remember the French that I studied in school.

We were not bothered by the German soldiers until our last day on the train. One of them came into the baggage car to just look around. He walked up to me and said, *"Donner du feu."* I thought surely my escape was over because I did not understand what he said and he glared at me. Monsieur immediately came over and struck a match to light the soldier's cigarette. I should have seen the cigarette hanging out of his mouth and realized he was only telling me to light it.

When we arrived at *la gare* (the train station) in Lille, my two helpers introduced me to Mademoiselle Rosa, who would take me to a safe house outside the city. Rosa, like Madame and Monsieur, was from Tunis and spoke French with a strange dialect and English with an odd accent. The Madame and Monsieur immediately got back on the train as it was departing. It happened so fast that I did not even have a chance to thank them. Rosa assured me that it was not necessary because they understood what I wanted to say to them.

Rosa and I went by taxi to a house outside of Lille and she introduced me to three men in the safe house. I remember the name of only one, "La Pipe" (pronounced "la peep" and meaning "the pipe"). In later years, when I was involved with clandestine intelligence work, I took "La Pipe" as my code name in memory of some wonderful French people who helped me return to England and thus saved my life. La Pipe spoke English with an American accent and the others spoke no English, so I spent most of my time with La Pipe.

My new helpers took me to a small bistro and we all ate our dinner in the kitchen so we would not be seen by the customers, most of whom were German soldiers. As we were walking back to the safe house, I bumped into a big German soldier walking in the opposite direction. He had a rifle slung over one shoulder and appeared to be drunk. Probably the wine I had with my dinner made me feel brave because I said, *"Excusez moi, monsieur,"* and just kept on walking. After we got out of hearing of the German, La Pipe, in a fit of laughter, had to lean up against a tree for support. He told me, *"Tu parles bien le Francais."* We both had a good laugh about an American escapee getting away with speaking French to a German soldier.

When we returned to the safe house, La Pipe showed me a room in which weapons were stacked like cord wood. He told me the rifles, machine guns, and pistols had been dropped to the underground by allied planes. Since they were all still in some type of a heavy dark preservative and no one in their group knew how to take them apart to clean them, they were not able to use them to kill Germans. Looking over the weapons, I saw they were mostly U.S. weapons. I told La Pipe that maybe now I could repay them, in a small way, for their help because I had been trained as a weapons specialist.

La Pipe called the others into the room and explained to them what I had said. There were lots of *"tres bons"* as I started to take apart a .45-caliber automatic. I then taught them how to field-strip, clean, and reassemble a .45-caliber automatic. We cleaned about six of those weapons. Using the same method, I taught them how to do the same thing with a machine gun and a carbine. We must have cleaned over a hundred weapons that night. They all became very adept at the field-stripping, cleaning, and reassembling of the weapons.

During the next few days we cleaned all of the U.S. weapons in that room. The last day of weapon cleaning, I became very ill and thought it was probably from the solvent we used for cleaning the weapons. La Pipe sent for a doctor.

After examining my head wound, the doctor became very concerned when he found the piece of flak still imbedded in my skull. When I told him it was from a flak wound about three months before, he became much more concerned. He applied a salve, bandaged the wound with a sterile dressing, and told La

Pipe I must to be sent to an American hospital immediately. Just when I was beginning to feel I was back as part of the war effort against the Germans. But I knew the doctor was right. I hurt all over and knew that I needed medical attention.

Early the next morning, after breakfast, La Pipe and I started on a long truck and train trip that took us to Bailleul, St. Omer, and finally to Calais. At Calais, I was placed in the care of a French fisherman. La Pipe helped me onto the boat and made me as comfortable as possible on a bunk. The fisherman told me, through La Pipe, "We will cross the Straits of Dover to Hythe, England, where I will put you in the care of the English." While we were still in the Straits of Dover, I must have passed out because I remember very little from that time until I woke up in the 303rd General Hospital.

The morning I awoke in a lucid state I learned the doctors had operated on my head the same day I arrived at the hospital—four days earlier. I realized later that, in preparing me for the operation, they had shaved my head and my beard but left my mustache.

The nurse went to get the surgeon when she found that I was awake. The doctor sat down next to my bed to explain the operation he had performed. He told me, "When we got you on the operating table I could easily tell the flak wound in your head was very dangerously close to becoming gangrenous." He smiled and said, "We usually have to amputate when gangrene is present, but in your case we decided that was not the thing to do." I sure didn't feel like listening to jokes, so I just replied, "I'm glad."

The doctor informed me it was necessary to take out a small section from the front of my skull and insert a silver plate, about the size of a quarter. "You'll probably have headaches, but there is medication to take care of the pain," he said. In a much more serious tone he added, "You are a very lucky young man. In another day or so it would have been too late for me to do anything for you." He then patted me on the shoulder and said, "I'll look in on you every day, but you have a special nurse assigned to you because you are not to get out of that bed for at least a month."

When the nurse, whose name was Helen, came back in, I asked her, "How can I shave and shower if I'm not permitted to get out of bed for a month?"

"It's very critical to your recovery that you stay in that bed. I'll take care of you until the doctor says you can get up and move around," she replied.

I asked Helen if she would help me grow an RAF-type mustache when she shaved me. She agreed.

Two weeks after my operation, the doctor permitted five people from Army intelligence to debrief me about my imprisonment, interrogation, abusive treatment, how I escaped, and who helped me after I got away. Their last question of that day was, "During your interrogations, what information did you give to the Germans?"

My reply was, "Name, rank, and serial number until they started beating me up and pulling my teeth. After that I just did not answer their questions." I told the intelligence people I could not identify the people who helped me escape because, if I was given a name it was only a first name or a code name and there were so many in both Belgium and France. I also told them that, in order to escape, I killed the German guard who had killed Pete the first night after we became prisoners of war.

The major who was in charge of the intelligence team said, "Lieutenant, you only did what had to be done. Don't dwell on it or even allow yourself to think about the incident. I'm sure the Army will have ways of telling you what a great job you did. I just want to shake your hand and, as one officer to another, say to you, well done."

Two days after the intelligence people debriefed me, our group CO, Colonel Burns, and my squadron CO, Maj. Frank Richardson, came to visit me.

Colonel Burns said, "I read the intelligence report about what you went through and I've been authorized to present you with the Silver Star Medal for gallantry in action. By resisting German interrogation and escaping from your captors, you reflected great credit on yourself and the 351st Bomb Group." He pinned the Silver Star Medal on my pajama shirt, and Major Richardson pinned on another Purple Heart Medal. Frank also gave me my old A-2 jacket, which he had retrieved for me.

Colonel Burns continued, "On the day you were shot down, the rest of the formation reported that your aircraft blew up and there were no chutes. I'm sorry but you were all reported as KIA (killed in action). No one knew that you and Pete had been captured. The records for all of you were retired, but we have taken steps to have yours reactivated and the Red Cross has been instructed to notify your family."

When I asked Frank who had my A-2 jacket, he smiled and said, "Don't ask." I didn't ask because I was so glad to get it back.

It has always been a mystery why flying personnel develop such an attachment to their A-2 jackets, almost like a love affair with a beautiful woman. Whenever someone was reported as KIA or MIA (missing in action), all his friends helped themselves to his flying gear and anything that was not locked up tight. It may seem heartless and immoral, but that's the way it was done in combat.

It was with great sadness that I learned from Major Richardson that my friend Robbie and his entire crew were killed in Scotland. Their airplane crashed into a mountain on their way back to the States after completing their combat tour.

After Colonel Burns and Major Richardson left, the doctor came back into my room and told me, "If you can gain back some weight and get some meat on your bones, you should be able to go back to the States in a week or ten days. Meanwhile, you are still not to get out of bed until I give you the word. I'm sure you are not aware of it, but the day of your operation you weighed ninety-seven pounds, even though your medical records showed your regular weight ran about one-thirty-five. You've only gained back one pound since your operation, but that was expected. I really think the best medication that I could prescribe for you would be to send you back to your family in the States with a ninety-day R and R leave. However, you need to gain at least two more pounds before we can do that."

I asked the doctor, "How did you know who I was when I was brought into the hospital? The Germans took my dog tags and all of my other identification—even my crash bracelet."

"You have teeth in your mouth that were made for you by the Army and the Army imbedded your name and serial number in the top of the plate." We both had a laugh about that, and he said, "That's the Army way."

After another week, I was finally allowed to get out of bed for the first time and encouraged to walk around with crutches as long as it did not cause too much pain. It was very tiresome and painful, but I forced myself to do it because I knew I wouldn't get out of there until I was ambulatory.

Helen went with me on my walks and was very supportive in my recovery attempt. Keeping her promise to help me grow an

RAF-type mustache, she found a baby hairbrush and would sit by my bed for hours, just brushing that mustache until it was thick and had a natural upward curl. Now that I was allowed out of bed she gave me the brush and said I could now take care of my own mustache.

The day finally arrived when I weighed in at 100 pounds. Before he discharged me from the hospital, the doctor gave me three different prescription pills to relieve headaches. He explained to me, "One is for a frontal headache, one if the pain is behind your eyes, and one if the headache is at the top of your head." When I asked how long I would need the pills, he just shrugged and said, "You're young enough that you will probably outgrow the pain."

On the day I was to leave, Helen and the doctor walked me to the front of the hospital. I thanked them both for all they had done for me, and I especially thanked the doctor for giving me back my life. A hospital staff car took me to town, where I boarded a train for London. The other passengers and I just stayed in the same car when we reached London and the car was attached to the *Royal Scot,* which was headed for Preswick, Scotland.

We learned that Col. Jimmy Stewart, the movie star, was the commanding officer of the bomb group at Preswick. I went out to the ballpark one day just to watch him play in a softball game while I was waiting for assignment to a crew. Hundreds of B-17s at Preswick were waiting to be flown back to the States by make-up crews, and I was assigned as the bombardier on one such crew. Our aircraft had bomb bay fuel tanks, so we flew direct from Preswick, Scotland, to Bangor, Maine. When we landed at Bangor, it was difficult for me to move, but when I got out of that airplane with the crew, we got down on all fours to kiss the earth of the good old USA. The only trouble was that I had to have help in getting back up on my feet (I was still using a cane). I decided not to try that again for a while.

Our processing was very quick, probably because everyone on the crew had been wounded during their combat tour and we had just completed a nonstop flight from Preswick. Part of the processing was to bring our pay up to date. I had not been paid since I was shot down, which meant I had about six months' pay and allowances due. I was loaded with over $3,000. Not much now, but then it was a small fortune.

We were all given railroad tickets to our hometowns and a bus ride into the city to catch our trains. I was very fortunate because the train for Cincinnati pulled out just fifteen minutes after I got on board. The crew members I came home with were scheduled on different trains to different hometowns. Since I didn't know anyone on the train, I just stayed to myself so I could read and sleep all the way to Cincinnati.

Silver Star

CHAPTER 15

Home at Last

On that beautiful Sunday morning, May 5, 1945, the Union Station in Cincinnati, Ohio, was similarly beautiful to me. Just three years before, I had departed from that city to begin my big adventure. Now I was home at last.

A red cap helped me down the steps from the railcar and said he would carry my bags to the curb. Halfway to the front of the station, I had to sit down and rest a few minutes. It was hard for me to realize that I was still so weak. The red cap sat down next to me and said, "Are you hurting, Lieutenant? Can I get you a drink of water or something?"

I replied, "I'll be fine after I rest a few minutes, but I appreciate your concern."

When we got to the front of the station, the taxi driver loaded my bags in the trunk and I gave him the address of my grandmother's house. As I settled into the seat of that cab, I said, "It sure is great to be home."

"Been gone long, Lieutenant?" the cabbie asked. "You sure look like you've seen a lot of action."

"Three years," I said, "but it seems like a lifetime."

En route to Hyde Park, we passed many areas that were very familiar to me from my teenage days. Those were places where we went to dances, the roller skating rink, my favorite hamburger joints, neighborhoods where my friends lived, etc. I just leaned my head back against the seat and drank it all in as I reminisced.

Arriving at my grandmother's house, the cabbie wanted to carry my bags in for me, but I just had him put them on the curb and paid him for the ride. Walking up to the house I noticed a

Gold Star Flag in the window and thought they should have taken that down when they found out I was still alive.

I stepped up onto the porch, opened the door, and walked into the hallway. To my left was the living room, and my whole family—aunts, uncles and cousins—were seated there. The men just stared. The women screamed, and my aunt Verna passed out on the sofa. The kids, my little cousins, ran from the room. There was just plain pandemonium in that house until everyone finally realized it was really me standing there, propped against my cane, with sunken cheeks and an RAF mustache. My grandmother came in from the kitchen to see what all the noise was about, and she was the calmest one of them all. She put her arms around me and said, "Oh, Junior, I just knew you would come back home."

When everyone finally settled down, the kids all came back into the room and all three wanted to sit next to me. I had to get out of the chair and sit on the floor. Everybody began talking at once, and I learned that the Red Cross had neglected to notify my family that I was not dead and was in an American hospital. My uncle Russell brought me a plaque from the mantle over the fireplace. My bomb group had sent it to my grandmother a couple of weeks after she received the telegram from the War Department. The plaque had a small Purple Heart Medal in the middle. Across the top was my name and bomb group number, and at the bottom were the rather stark words: "Killed in action 23 December 1944" (the wrong date). Reading that plaque gave me a chill that the Germans had been unable to cause. I was glad I was sitting down.

Uncle Russell motioned to me to go to the kitchen with him. I tried to get off the floor but could not make it, so he came over and helped me to my feet. In the kitchen Russ said to me, "Your dad got married again and is living in Oakley. Do you want me to call him?" I told him not until later.

When we returned to the living room, the kids had all gone outside to tell the neighborhood kids that I was back home. The little boy next door, who was three years old when I went away, came over to see me, took one look at my sunken face and my big bushy mustache, let out a scream, and took off for home. I went upstairs and shaved off the mustache and went back to the living room. Everyone agreed they were glad I shaved "that thing" off my face.

They were bombarding me with hundreds of questions, but I got Russ off to the side and asked him, "Will you please tell

everyone I just don't want to talk about it now and I really do need some rest?"

He did that individually and then told me, "I sure would like to hear all about your adventure, but only when you are ready."

"OK, Russ. But in America and in my family, I am still just a kid and I doubt if anyone would believe it if I told them what I have been through."

Russ wanted to know, "What makes you think that?"

"I flew thirty-seven combat missions, made four crash landings, bailed out of a burning aircraft, was wounded twice, was a prisoner-of-war, then escaped by myself, and made my way back with the help of some wonderful and courageous people in the Belgium and French underground. Until my birthday, three days ago, in my own country, I still could not vote or legally buy an alcoholic drink. And just a little while ago, my dear grandmother called me Junior."

"I see what you mean," Russ said, "but I recognize those medals and you are certainly a man in my eyes."

Even though it was early in the evening, I just had to go up to my bedroom to get some sleep.

When I awoke on my first day at home, I got on the bathroom scales to see if I had gained any weight on my trip home. Looking down at the dial, it read 101 pounds. The doctor told me that regaining my strength and weight would be a lengthy task. Now I believed him.

I went downstairs in my pajamas and robe and found that my grandmother and aunt Verna had a huge breakfast waiting for me. I was able to eat everything they put in front of me without any rumbling feeling in my stomach. The family cat came into the kitchen and kept rubbing up against my legs. Perhaps I could have learned something from her about relaxing, because I felt as though my whole body was wound up as tight as a clock spring. Grandmother and Verna sat with me as I enjoyed my breakfast. It was obvious that they had hundreds of questions, but they had acceded to my request for everyone to refrain from asking any questions.

Grandmother, in her loving way, said, "I am so happy to have you back home. My nightly prayers for your safe return have been answered. I just could not believe the telegram I received from the War Department that said you had been killed on a bombing mission. When the folks at church heard about the telegram, they brought me the Gold Star Mothers flag and I just hung it in the front window. You'll notice it has now been replaced by an American flag." She paused. "I understand that Russell told you your father remarried and is living in Oakley." When I nodded, she said, "I called him to tell him you had returned, and he will be over to see you tonight with his new wife. I hope you don't mind my calling him." I shrugged, smiled, and said, "I knew you would, but my feelings have not changed."

After breakfast, I went upstairs, shaved, showered, and put on a clean uniform. Back downstairs, I telephoned my good friend, Johnny Meents. He asked, "Are you at your grandmother's?" All I got out of my mouth was yes and he said, "Stay there, I'll be right over." I went out to the porch swing and allowed my mind to wander to happier and healthier times.

Three minutes after my phone call, Johnny drove up honking his horn. I hobbled out to the curb with my cane to meet him. We shook hands and then bear hugged each other. I don't remember his first words exactly, but I think he said, "Man, you look like hell but I'm glad you're back home, almost in one piece."

We sat in the porch swing to talk about old times, and Grandmother brought us a pot of coffee and some homemade cookies. Johnny wanted to know what my plans were and I told him, "I've decided on a military career in the Army Air Forces." He didn't appear too surprised at my answer.

Johnny had a class at the University of Cincinnati that afternoon and I asked him to drop me off at Hyde Park Square on his way. When I got there, I took a seat on a bench and glanced around, noticing a large monument inscribed with rows and rows of names. Upon closer examination I found it had been erected by the people of Hyde Park, in honor of the boys from the area who were in the service. A gold star denoted those killed in the war. Next to my name was a gold star. I took out my pocketknife and scraped it off the monument. Somehow, it seemed like an important thing for me to do.

My next stop was at my friend George Runte's hardware store, where I had spent several happy summers delivering small packages and practicing my driving in George's four-door Plymouth sedan. He still thought that I had been killed in action, so there was pandemonium in the store when I walked through the door. George ran over with tears streaming down his face and grabbed me with a big hug. Many of the customers in the store remembered me and came over to shake hands. The customers who did not know me probably wondered what kind of mad house they had walked into that day.

After all the greetings and handshaking, things settled down and George told his two clerks that he and I were going next door for coffee and a Danish.

When we had our coffee and Danish in front of us, George said, "I want to hear all about your adventure." I took a sip of my coffee and said I just didn't care to talk about it now, and I hoped he understood. George replied, "I do understand because I felt the same way when I came home from World War I. However, you will have to get it out of your system someday and I will be here to listen. Just don't wait too long."

George had been in France during World War I, as a major in the Army Engineers. Several years before, he had told me how his life was saved by a French family when the Germans overran the location he was in with two other engineers. The French family hid them in their basement until the Germans were driven out of the area.

When we had finished our third cup of coffee and second Danish, I told George I was going to hop on a streetcar and take a trip to downtown Cincinnati. He wouldn't hear of that and handed me his car keys.

"You'll be wanting to visit girlfriends and other friends, so you take my car and use it as long as you are home," he said. "There are gasoline ration coupons in the glove compartment, and if you'll come by tomorrow, I'll take you to the War Ration Office up the street and get you a returning soldier ration coupon book." He said he now had a pickup truck for deliveries and could use it while I had his car.

After thanking him, I hobbled on my cane out to his Plymouth, the same one I had used to learn to drive and make deliveries in before I left for the war. Heading for the downtown area, I drove through Oakley, Norwood, Bond Hill, and finally the downtown area. I was reminiscing all the way. Fountain Square, with the many rippling waterfalls, was just as beautiful as I remembered. I stopped at the Barn, a favorite watering hole for my friends, but it was too early to find it open. Leaving there, I went to the Purple Cow, another favorite place for my friends, and had a hamburger, French fried onions, and a milkshake. There were crowds of people everywhere but no one I knew, so I left the downtown area.

I remembered that Montgomery Avenue used to be loaded with used car dealers, so I headed for that area, intending to use some of my back pay to purchase a used car because new ones were not yet being manufactured. I looked at numerous autos on several different lots until I found one that appeared to be in very good condition. It was a 1940 cherry red Ford two-door coupe with a tan leather interior and whitewall tires—the prettiest thing on any of the lots. The total price was $699. I gave the man $100 to hold it for me until the next day. That $699 for an auto was the biggest purchase I had ever made.

Going back to Hyde Park, I went by the hardware store en route to Grandmother's house. I told George I would be picking up the car I purchased the next day. He said, "You sure don't waste time. Just take the Plymouth home with you. Come by the store in the morning after ten o'clock and I'll take you to town to pick up your car."

Grandmother was sitting in the swing on the front porch, shelling peas, and when she saw me drive up in the light green Plymouth she said, "I see you have been visiting with your friend, George Runte."

I sat down on the swing to help her shell the peas and said, "Johnny Meents and George are the only friends I have seen so far. We went to the Tea Room and had George's favorite, coffee and a Danish."

She laughed and said, "Everyone in Hyde Park knows that's his favorite morning and afternoon snack."

"George wanted me to use his car while I was home, Grandmother, but there are a couple of families I want to visit in Texas and Kansas. So I went out on Montgomery Avenue and bought my own car." I told her about Pete being killed when we tried to escape the first night after we were captured and about Robbie, our squadron bombardier, being killed when he crashed in Scotland on his way back to the States.

"I remember you writing to me about both of them, Bill," she said. "I'm so sorry to hear they were both killed. I assume you are going to visit their families."

"Yes, I'll leave the first part of next week, after I get used to driving my car around the city. Pete's family lives in Port Arthur, Texas, and Robbie's family lives in Salina, Kansas. That would be a great distance to drive in a borrowed car."

Grandmother told me that my dad and Virginia would be over for dinner around 6:30, so I went upstairs to take a shower and put on a clean uniform. Since military personnel were still required to wear uniforms unless engaged in sports, I still did not have any civilian clothes.

When my father and Virginia arrived, I shook hands with Virginia and put out my hand to shake hands with my father. He grabbed me and hugged me with tears in his eyes. That was the first and only affection I ever remember receiving from my father, but it sure broke the ice that night. He wanted to know what all the medals were and how I won them, but he had obviously been told I did not want to talk about my experiences.

Grandmother's dinner was delicious, as usual, and there was much light talk at the table. Everyone was interested in the trip I planned to take to Texas and Kansas. Virginia asked, "Aren't you afraid to take such a long trip?"

I just smiled and told her, "No, after where I've been, it will be like a trip to the grocery store."

I told my father about the car I bought and he said he would look it over for me before I left on my trip. I was glad he made that offer, because he always worked on his own car and many of his friends always asked him to work on their cars. He said, "Why don't you come over to the house for dinner tomorrow night and we'll check it out thoroughly?"

After dinner, while we were sitting around in the living room, I suddenly began to feel very weak. It occurred to me that I had forgotten to take my medication, which I did immediately. The excitement of the day had probably been too much for me. I excused myself and went to bed.

The next morning, I picked up George at 10:30 and he took me to the auto dealer on Montgomery Avenue. The dealer had my car sitting in front of his office, all washed and ready to go. George and I looked it over and he pointed out that it looked like the dealer had the car waxed. I paid the man six $100 bills. He gave me the title to the car and $1.00. He also gave me a thirty-day guarantee that if anything went wrong with the car it would be taken care of, free of charge. I thanked George for bringing me down, and he departed.

On the way back to Hyde Park in my red Ford, I stopped in Bond Hill to see Roberta, the girl that I had dated quite often while we were in high school. She was in her last year at the University of Cincinnati and had just gotten home from school. She could not believe it when she finally recognized me and told me, "All the gang heard you had been killed on a bombing mission. I'm so glad to see you, and I know the rest our friends will be happy to know you are home safe! So will my parents! They're both in Atlanta today." She hugged and kissed me and said, "Why are we standing out on the porch? Come in the house."

Roberta brought me up to date on what had been going on in Cincinnati during the past three years. She told me about a dance at the University Club on Friday night and said all the gang would be there. When she hinted that she didn't have a date, I asked her if she planned to go and she said, "What time would you like to pick me up?" When I suggested we have dinner somewhere first and then go to the dance, she said, "Just like old times?"

"Not quite," I answered. "In my present physical condition, you'll probably have to do most of your dancing with some other guys."

After my fourth cup of coffee, I told her that I was due at my father's house for dinner and had better head for home to shower and change. I asked her, "Would six be a good time to pick you up for dinner Friday?"

She nodded. "I'll be looking forward to Friday night."

"Me too," I said, and took off for home in my cherry red Ford.

When I arrived at Grandmother's, I had dozens of phone calls from friends who had just found out I was back home and not dead. It occurred to me that Roberta must have gotten busy on the phone after I left her house. I sat down at the phone bench and started dialing. Most of them said they planned to be at the dance on Friday night and would look forward to seeing me again. I finally got off the phone, showered, changed uniforms, and headed for dinner at my father's house.

While Virginia prepared dinner, my father brought out his tools, meters, and other equipment and gave my auto a thorough checking over. He told me the car was in excellent condition. When I said I got it for $700, he told me I had gotten a very good buy.

During a nice dinner, the conversation was very friendly. While Virginia was clearing off the table, my father and I moved into the living room. He asked me if I would like to go to federal court with him the next day. It seemed the government was suing him to make him accept my life insurance policy payoff of $10,000 because he was the beneficiary and I was officially declared dead.

I said, "That might be fun. I'll pick you up in the morning." After thinking for a while I asked him, "Why did you not accept the money? I was officially declared dead and you would be $10,000 ahead." His response really surprised me when he said, "I always felt there was a chance that you would come home as long as I didn't take the money." He continued, "I know that I wasn't much of a father to you while you were growing up, and I regret that. I hope, now that we are both men, we can be friends."

"I'd sure like that, Dad, and this would be a good time to start," I told him. I didn't know that my father was emotional, but he had tears in his eyes.

Virginia brought in a tray with scotch, bourbon, ice, and glasses. When she asked if I would like a drink, I told her, "The medication the doctors have me taking does not permit mixing it with alcohol, but I sure could drink one beer." She went to the kitchen and returned with a beer.

We played cards for a while and then I had to excuse myself because I felt I might go to sleep at the wheel if I did not leave. I thanked Virginia for the dinner and told my father I would pick him up at 10:00 A.M.

At breakfast, my grandmother and Verna asked about my dinner last night. I told them about Dad pronouncing my auto a very good buy, about going to court with him that morning, and about the talk he and I had about being friends.

Grandmother dried her eyes and said, "I'm so glad to hear that. You never had a father when you were growing up, but maybe you both can make up for all that lost time."

I picked up my father at 10:00 and we headed for the federal courthouse. When my father's case was called, the judge asked him why he had not accepted the money from the federal government. I walked up and stood beside him and said, "Because I am not dead, your honor. I was originally reported as killed when my aircraft blew up, but I bailed out and was captured by the Germans. My bomb group did not know I was still alive until I escaped and got back to England three months later. I'm sorry to have caused so much trouble for the court."

The judge replied, "You have not caused trouble for this court, Lieutenant. I just thank God you are home alive and I'm sure your family feels the same way. Case dismissed." The judge then came down from his bench, shook my hand, and said, "Welcome home, Lieutenant." That really choked me up. I had to get out of there before I did something really stupid like cry.

After I took Dad home, I stopped at a florist to pick up a gardenia corsage for Roberta and some roses for my grandmother, then went home. After a shave and shower, I put on a neatly pressed uniform with shined shoes and headed for Roberta's house.

She met me at the door, dressed in a long skirt, sweater, bobby socks, and saddle oxfords. Suddenly, it seemed we had turned the clock back three years. Then I looked down at my uniform and returned to reality. She didn't have any preference for dinner so we went to Frisches, one of the well-known hangouts.

When we arrived at the University Club, the dance had already started and the band was playing "Stardust." I laid my cane on an empty table and we danced to the end of that number. As we were leaving the dance floor, dozens of friends, including Johnny Meents and his date, saw us and almost carried us to the large table they had reserved. Roberta lost her corsage in the rush and I went back to look for it. Someone had picked it up and placed it on a table where I had left my cane. I picked up both and went back to our table. Roberta whispered to me that she had told everyone not to ask me anything about the war unless I started to talk about my experiences. All I could say was, "I appreciate your thoughtfulness."

All the guys wanted to know what I planned to do when the war was over. Johnny spoke up and told them, "He's staying in the Army."

"Yes, I've already decided on a military career in the Army Air Forces," I told them. "I hope to go back to flying when I get my strength back, and I plan to get my degree by going to college during my off-duty time."

One of the fellows said, "That's heavy stuff, Bill. When did you learn to make decisions like that?"

"I don't know, I guess the Army taught me."

A wonderful evening with good friends finally came to an end when the band began playing "Good Night, Ladies." That made four dances I got up for that night. I would never have believed I could do it, and Roberta kept asking if I was getting too tired. She was very understanding about me not being able to dance too much. We said good night to our friends, and I gathered phone numbers from the guys who wanted to get together when I returned from my trip to Texas and Kansas.

When we got to Roberta's house, she said, "I wish you could come to my graduation." I told her I'd certainly like to do that but, even though I had a ninety-day leave, I was subject to being called back at any time—and that trip was something I just had to do. She said, "I understand."

I thought to myself that if I ever wanted to settle down, she was the type of girl I would want to settle down with. She asked me to call her when I got back from my trip and I told her I'd send her postcards along the way and call her as soon as I got back. We kissed good night and I headed for home.

The next day being a Saturday, I went to see my sister at Aunt Florence's house, where she was living at the time. I learned that she was due to graduate from Hughes High School in another month, and I told her how proud I was of her for sticking it out. I explained to her about not being able to attend her graduation, as I had explained to Roberta. Then I took her out for a milkshake and a ride in my red Ford.

CHAPTER 16

My Quest

Pete and Robbie were closer to me in wartime than any family member, and in my mind, visiting their families was a duty that could not be ignored if I was to ever have peace of mind.

With maps from a local service station, I did my route planning just as for mission planning – a leg at a time. My first leg would be from Cincinnati to Salina, Kansas, on U.S. Route 50. From Salina to Port Arthur, Texas, and then back home. The distance of the round trip came to about 2,300 miles. After drawing my route on the maps and adding up the mileage again, I decided I was just not strong enough yet to attempt to drive 2,300 miles. It would be wiser if I took the train.

Monday morning, after a big breakfast with Grandmother and Aunt Verna, I called a taxi to take me to Union Station. When I made my reservations on Saturday, I was told I could pick up my tickets an hour before departure time. Since I had Pullman car reservations, I would be in the same car to Kansas City. Upon arriving at Kansas City, there was a long delay for a train to Salina. So I decided to get a rebate on the rest of my train tickets and make reservations a leg at a time for the rest of the journey.

The red cap who stood with me while I got my ticket rebate told me, "I live in Salina and I've always found the Greyhound bus was the best way from Kansas City to Salina." He carried my bags to the front of the station and hailed a cab for me. When I arrived at the bus terminal I got four dollars' worth of change from the ticket seller and went to a phone to call Sioux City. I had promised Jean I would go to see her when I returned from the war. From Kansas City to Sioux City was only about 100 miles, but I thought I had better call first.

Jean's mother answered the phone. She had a hard time believing it was really me. "The Christmas package Jean sent to you in early December and the letter she sent on Christmas day both came back marked 'killed in action'," she said. "Jean was really broken up and cried most of the time. Last March, she and a couple of her friends went to San Francisco to work in one of the defense plants. They all seem to like California, and Jean is engaged to be married next month."

I asked about Jack and his father and learned they were both well. Jack had gone back to school under the GI Bill after his discharge from the Navy.

Jean's mother said, "I'm very sorry things did not work out for you and Jean because I always thought you two made such a nice couple."

The first call for the bus to Salina was announced, so I asked Jean's mother to give my best wishes to everyone and hung up the phone. I was glad that Jean had found happiness in California. I decided that she was a pleasant chapter in my life that was now over.

Arriving at Salina at 11:00 on a very pleasant summer morning, I stopped to telephone Robbie's parents. His mother answered the phone. I said, "This is Lt. Bill Cramer . . . Robbie and I served together . . ."

She stopped me in midsentence and said, "Bill, Robbie wrote so much about you to us that we feel we have known you for years. But last December, Robbie sent me a very sad letter telling me that you had been killed on a bombing raid over Belgium."

I told her the purpose of my trip to Salina and to Port Arthur, Texas. "Would it be convenient for me to come out to meet you and Mr. Robinson?"

"It sure is convenient and you must plan to spend a few days with us before going to Texas."

I told her I was calling from the bus terminal and asked directions to their house. "You just go in the coffee shop and my husband will be there within twenty minutes. How will he know you?"

My answer was, "I'm the only skinny lieutenant with a cane that I've seen here."

As I was having my second cup of coffee, Robbie's father walked up to my table, stuck out his hand, and said, "I'm Bob Robinson and you have to be the Bill Cramer we heard so much about from our Robbie."

As we shook hands I replied, "I hope what Robbie told you was not all bad."

Bob sat down to have a cup of coffee while I finished mine and said, "Robbie told us you were his best friend, one of the best young men that America had to offer . . . that you flew every mission you could in spite of being shot down four times. He also told us you shot down two German fighters."

That choked me up a little and I said, "I had the pleasure of serving with your son for only a short time, but I found him to be a good friend, a fine officer, an excellent bombardier, and a brave flier. You have every right to be proud of him."

"Thank you, Bill," he replied, "we are very proud of him and his fellow fliers, especially men like you who would travel such a distance just to visit with the family of a lost comrade."

After finishing our coffee, Bob retrieved my bags and led me outside to his white Lincoln Continental. When I commented on the beautiful condition of the car, he told me he had owned it since before the war started and that it had performed without a problem. I leaned back into that soft, natural-colored leather and really enjoyed the trip to the Robinsons' home.

Approaching the house by way of the long, tree-lined circular drive was a peaceful sight. The house was an elegant two-story white colonial with tall pillars and a large front porch, where Mrs. Robinson was awaiting our arrival. I was introduced to the very charming lady who insisted her name was Mary Robinson, not Mrs. Robinson.

Mary called Sam, their houseman, and asked him to take my bags to the guest room. Before taking my bags, Sam came over and shook my hand, "You must be Robbie's friend that he wrote so much about. I'm very happy to meet you."

Mary had iced tea waiting for us on the porch table, and we all sat down to get acquainted. She told me, "Sam's father was our houseman for twenty years, and Robbie and Sam played together when they were children. When Sam's father retired, Sam took his place. Robbie being killed in the war was a terrible loss to Sam also." She paused and then said, "Irene, Robbie's sister, went to the market and should be back shortly."

As soon as she said that, Irene drove up in a white Ford. After introductions, I helped Irene carry the groceries into the kitchen and Sam put them away. I put my hand on Sam's shoulder and said, "Robbie was my best friend, too, Sam. We both lost someone very special."

Sam replied, "Yes, sir, we sure did."

Irene and I went back to the porch to join her parents. I mentioned to them that Irene's white Ford was a twin to my red Ford. Irene said her dad got the car for her when she started college at the University of Kansas three years ago. She asked, "Did your dad buy yours for you?"

"No, after being a prisoner of war, Uncle Sam owed me so much money I decided to spend some of it for a car. I really intended to drive out here to see you folks and then go to Texas to see the parents of another friend I used to fly with frequently. After I mapped out the trip and saw how far it was, I decided to take the train."

Bob spoke up and said, "The driving time would have used over two weeks of valuable time you could spend in better pursuits. Besides, I can see you have not completely regained your strength after your ordeal."

"The day after I arrived home, I got on the scales and only weighed a hundred and one pounds, when my normal weight is one-thirty," I told him.

Mary spoke up. "I have several friends who would love to be able to say they weigh a hundred and one pounds."

I told them about the dance I attended where I went in using my cane but was able to dance four slow dances. Then Irene said, "My sorority is having a dance in Wichita Saturday night. Would you like to go?" I told her that I would have liked that very much, but I had to leave before Saturday.

Mary went inside to see about dinner and Bob left for his office, so Irene said, "Let's go for a ride." Her mother told us not to be gone more than four hours because dinner would be on the table by 7:00 P.M.

Like every other American city, Salina had a favorite hangout for its youth. The hangout there was the Tee-Pee, a large hamburger joint. When we walked in, it seemed that everyone in the place knew Irene and came over to speak to her and to meet her "date" for the afternoon. Irene introduced me to everybody as one of Robbie's friends who flew combat with him. Apparently not many military people had been seen in Salina, and all the girls wanted to finger my wings and ribbons and asked what each ribbon was for. Irene knew the names of the ribbons and answered their questions.

The juke box was playing the songs that were popular when I left for the war, and it sure did bring back fond memories.

After leaving the Tee-Pee, we drove around town to see and be seen. It didn't take long because Salina, Kansas, was not that large of a town. Finally Irene said, "Let's go by my dad's place."

We drove up to a large Lincoln dealership and went inside. There was only one car on the floor of the showroom – a 1941 black Lincoln in mint condition.

Bob came out of his office and said, "Would you like to purchase a Lincoln?"

I asked, "On a lieutenant's pay?"

He laughed and told me, "You won't always be a lieutenant." When I said I hoped he was right, he smiled and said, "I know I'm right, so come see me when you're ready for a Lincoln. You will have your choice at my cost." I thanked him for his kind offer, and he took us out to show what he had on his used car lot. He told me, "It will probably be a year after the war is over before we get any new cars, so we exist by selling used cars."

Bob said he had some paperwork to finish before going home, so Irene and I departed. Since it was getting close to dinner time, we went back to her house.

Irene showed me around the estate, including the stables. She took me up to one of the stalls and pointed out the horse that Robbie bought as a colt the year before he went into the Army Air Corps. It was a beautiful pinto, and the sign on the stall door identified him as "Ace." She told me, "Dad is the only one who rides him now that Robbie is gone." She then showed me her strawberry roan named Irish. There were several other horses in the stable and Irene explained, "Dad lets some of my friends keep their horses here as long as they keep the place clean."

Bob had come home and was sitting on the front porch. After I got cleaned up, I joined him. He asked, "Did you and Irene enjoy your afternoon?"

My reply was, "Yes, she showed me all around town. It's very obvious to me that she misses Robbie very much."

"They were very close and Robbie was always her 'big brother'," Bob said. "His death has been very rough on all of us, but especially on Irene."

"It's strange how Robbie and I became so close," I said, "but, being six years older than me, he acted like a big brother to me also. He was always worried that I was flying too many combat missions on consecutive days.

"I especially remember one incident. Robbie was very short of lead bombardiers and I agreed to fly on three consecutive days to Munich. On the last mission our aircraft was shot up so badly, we had to crash land at another base that had a long grass strip at the end of the runway. It was a wheels-up landing, and we were all pretty shaken from the experience. Robbie was on the same mission and landed with no problem. But when he found out we had to crash land at another base, he, the squadron CO, and two other crew members who had been on the mission drove staff cars all the way to the base where we landed just to take us back to our home base. Robbie came running over to me and asking me if I was all right. Our squadron CO was doing the same thing with the rest of my crew members, and I thought at the time how much they looked like a pair of mother hens looking after their chicks. That's how Robbie was—a caring person who was respected by all who knew him."

Bob said, "Bill, you have no idea how much your saying that about Robbie means to me."

After a delicious dinner and very pleasant conversation, Irene left for a date. Mary, Bob, and I sat in rockers on the front porch. I could tell that Mary wanted to talk about Robbie. I told them about the day Robbie and I were having breakfast in the combat crew mess hall. Jeff, a pilot friend of Robbie's, had joined us and talked us into going up in his B-17 to do a slow roll just because everybody said it couldn't be done.

"After breakfast we took off in a B-17," I began, "just the three of us, and headed out over The Wash, where we usually got into formation before heading for our targets in Germany. We headed for The Wash because it was far enough from our base that no one would see us. We climbed up to 9,000 feet. Jeff was in the left seat, Robbie was in the right seat, and I stood between them. When they started rocking the aircraft, I went back to the radio operator's position and put on the seat belt. They kept getting closer and closer to a wingover. They got it in a position where one wing was pointing straight down and the ship fell off and went into a dive. We lost almost 8,000 feet in that dive, but they got it pulled out and climbed back up to 11,000 feet for another try.

"On the second try, their coordination was better and their rocking and rocking caused that big, beautiful B-17 to do a graceful slow roll. We then went back to the base and wore smug looks on our faces for the next few days." I paused, thinking about what we had done. "Many might consider that a stupid trick, but we considered it a beautiful feat of airmanship because it was not supposed to be possible."

Next Bob told me a story. "When Robbie was ten years old, I caught him on the roof of the stable with an umbrella, and he jumped off just as I yelled for him to get down off the roof. He broke his left wrist and decided he did not want to become a paratrooper after all."

I told Mary and Bob how much I had enjoyed my brief stay with them but I felt I should head for Texas the next day. Mary said they would love to have me stay longer, but she understood. She then asked, "Would you like to call your home to let them know your plans?" I told her I appreciated her offer because I needed to find out if my orders had been changed and to let my grandmother know my plans.

I talked with my grandmother and learned there had been no word from the Army, so I told her I would leave for Port Arthur, Texas, the next day and and then head for home. She told me I had had more than twenty phone calls since I had left.

When I went back to the porch, Bob told me, "You will have a better chance to get a train to Port Arthur in Wichita, so either Irene or I will take you there to make your connection." I told Bob how much I appreciated his offer, excused myself, and went to bed.

While we were having breakfast, Bob told Irene that I would be leaving for Port Arthur that day and he thought I would make better connections in Wichita. She replied, "Oh yes, it's hard to get anywhere by train from Salina. I'll drive him to Wichita." It was settled that quickly.

A couple of hours later, as I was thanking Mary and Bob for their hospitality, they both hugged me and thanked me for coming to see them and for being such a good friend to Robbie. I tossed my B-4 bag into Irene's car and we headed for Wichita. She was a very careful driver, so the 100-mile trip took us almost three hours.

At the train station, I found there was an express train leaving for Houston at 8:00 P.M., with no need to change trains, so I got a Pullman reservation. There was about a four-hour wait and I told Irene, "I'd like to take you to dinner if you don't mind driving back home after dark."

She told me, "I drive after dark every time I come home or go back to college, so I don't mind. And I know of a real good restaurant here." I suggested she might want to call her folks to let them know her plans. After she called home she told me, "Mom and Dad said to tell you they hope that you will visit us again and stay longer the next time." I told her I would like very much to do that.

After an enjoyable dinner, Irene took me back to the train station and we said our goodbyes. She said, "Bill, you have no idea how much your visit has meant to my parents and to me. Your efforts in making the trip, even in your weakened condition, will help us accept our loss with more dignity." She gave me a big hug and a kiss and we parted.

My Pullman reservation was a roomette, so I got on board, went to bed, and I did not awaken even when we pulled out of the station thirty minutes later.

From Wichita to Houston there were only two stops: Oklahoma City and Dallas. Oklahoma City must have been a smooth stop because I didn't even wake up when we pulled into the station. I was awake in time for a late breakfast in the diner when we arrived at Dallas. On my way back to my Pullman roomette I met a porter and asked him how long the trip was to Houston. He said, "On a good day we make the trip in five hours and on a bad day it takes as long as eight hours. I feel this is going to be a good day, Lieutenant, so if you have a late lunch in the diner we should be pulling into Houston about the time you finish. My name's Andy, and I'll help you off the train with your bag and get you a taxi out in front of the station." I thanked him for his information and his offer to help me with my bag.

Andy was right. We pulled into Houston just as I was about to order a scoop of ice cream for my luncheon dessert. I returned to the Pullman and Andy came by to take my bag. On the way to the front of the station, I must have been leaning heavily on my cane because Andy asked, "Does you leg give you much pain, Lieutenant?"

"It's my whole body that is giving me pain, Andy. I guess I am just trying to be too active too soon."

When we got to the taxi, I thanked Andy for his kindness and gave him a good tip. Andy gave me a big grin and said, "You have a good and safe trip, Lieutenant, and take it a little easier on yourself."

The taxi took me to the Greyhound bus terminal, where I bought a one-way ticket to Port Arthur. The 100-mile trip took three hours. I was surprised to see so much tropical vegetation in Texas. I almost felt as though I was back in Florida.

When I telephoned the home of Pete's parents, a man answered and identified himself as Paul Hagen.

"This is Lt. Bill Cramer. Are you Pete's father?"

"Yes . . . and I know a Bill Cramer from Pete's letters but he was supposed to have been shot down with Pete."

"Pete and I bailed out of the ship and we were captured by the Germans," I explained. "I just arrived in Port Arthur and, if it would not be inconvenient, I would like to come out to meet you and Mrs. Hagen."

After a pause he told me, "You must forgive me, Bill. Hearing from someone that Pete thought so much of and who we thought was also dead caused me to lose my sense of courtesy completely. Of course we want to see you. Tell me where you are and I'll come pick you up at once." When I said that I was at the bus terminal he told me he would pick me up in ten minutes.

Mr. Hagen drove up in a big, black Packard. He jumped out of the car almost before it was completely stopped and ran over to me with an outstretched hand. He kept saying how sorry he was for being so slow when I called. I told him, "It was really very stupid of me because you would have no way of knowing that I had escaped from the Germans."

He put my B-4 bag on the back seat, and we were on our way. Within fifteen minutes, we arrived at their beautiful home on the beach, overlooking the Gulf of Mexico. Mrs. Hagen came running out to the car and threw her arms around me.

"You are the first of Pete's combat friends that we have met, and he wrote to us about you so much," she said. "He worried about you flying so many combat missions in so short a period of time, and he told us about the two German fighters you shot down . . ."

Finally, Paul said, "Whoa, Ellen, the boy just got here. We'll have plenty of time to talk later." Then he asked, "Where do you hail from, Bill?"

"Cincinnati, but I came here from visiting the parents of another friend in Salina, Kansas."

Paul said sadly, "I guess he didn't make it home either."

"That's right," I answered. "Pete and Robbie were my best friends and I felt that a visit to their families would be the best way I could honor their memory, because I know I'll never forget them."

Ellen excused herself to get some refreshments, but I knew

she needed to dry her eyes as well. While she was gone I said, "Mr. Hagen—"

He interrupted me and said, "Bill, in Texas we call friends by their first name. I hope you will consider us your friends and call us Ellen and Paul."

"Roger. Before Ellen comes back I wanted to ask you how much I should say about Pete in front of her."

Paul said, "Ellen is a strong gal. She and I have accepted the fact that our only son gave his life in defense of what he and all Texans have always believed in—freedom. Ellen and I both have hundreds of questions, so don't feel that you have to hold anything back."

Ellen came back to the porch with a pitcher of iced tea and a big bowl of boiled shrimp. She sent Paul back into the house to get the ice, glasses, crackers, and a special sauce for the shrimp. With a smile, she told me, "Paul thinks he is the only one who can make shrimp sauce."

Paul came back to the porch pushing a tea cart with everything that was needed. I tried a shrimp with Paul's sauce and said, "I love shrimp and this is the very best sauce I have ever tasted. What brand is it?"

"I make it," he answered, "and if you like it I'll make up a batch so you can take some home with you."

I told Paul, "I have to confess, Ellen told me how proud you are of your shrimp sauce. But it really is the best shrimp sauce I have ever tasted. I'd love to take some home."

"I don't want you men to fill yourselves up with shrimp because I have the vegetables on the stove and you two can fix the steaks on the grill," Ellen said. Paul excused himself to go light the grill and advised us he could do that by himself.

"I thought we would have steaks at home tonight because you are probably tired after your long trip," Ellen said, and then asked, "Are you all right, Bill?"

"I guess I am a little tired, but I seem to stay tired most of the time. I sometimes wonder if I will ever regain my strength. The doctor told me it will take time, but he didn't say how much time."

Paul came back and asked me how I preferred my steak. I told him, "I remember Pete always wanted his steak at body temperature, but I prefer mine medium."

"Pete got that from his dad," Ellen said, "but I prefer mine medium also." She went into the house to do her part, and I went with Paul to do our part. We lounged in deck chairs under a large tree while the steaks simmered. It was such a peaceful setting. We had a wonderful dinner with very pleasant conversation.

After dinner, Ellen chased Paul and me out to the porch while she cleaned off the table. She would bring coffee as soon as it was brewed.

We sat in the large rocking chairs, with our feet up on the railing, looking out on the Gulf. There were a lot of small boats moving close to the beach, but we began to see a lot of ocean-going type vessels farther out.

"Most of those big ships are heading for Galveston because that is one of the largest ports on the Gulf," Paul said.

After surveying the scenery some more, I said, "It is so restful sitting here like this instead of flying in flak-filled skies."

Paul suddenly said, "Tell me about those flak-filled skies, Bill. Make me feel what my son felt when they were shooting at him."

"I don't know if I can do that, Paul, because the feeling a man gets in combat is a very personal thing and no two people feel the same. As a pilot, Pete had many duties that required his continuous attention while we were in enemy territory, and he may not have seen most of the flak. Even though I flew in the plexiglas nose, my duties kept me from seeing a lot of the flak that was bursting all around our aircraft."

Ellen brought out the coffee and joined us in a rocking chair. She was quiet for a spell and then said, "Bill, please tell us how our Pete died."

I looked at Paul and he nodded. "Well, Ellen, I was assigned to Pete's crew that day because a head cold had their regular bombardier grounded. Our target was in Belgium, and we were to bomb the German front lines to help relieve the pressure on our ground troops who were surrounded in what has become known as the Battle of the Bulge. After dropping our bombs, we took a direct hit, knocking our number-three engine completely out of the wing, and causing us to go into an inverted dive, with flames pouring out of the hole left by our missing engine. We went into a bank of clouds, with parts still falling off our aircraft, and that is probably the reason the rest of the formation reported that we blew up. However, after losing almost 13,000 feet in that dive, Pete and the other pilot were able to pull us out of the dive so that the men on our crew, who were left alive, were able to bail out."

Paul asked, "How high were you when you all bailed out?"

"I'm not sure, but I was the last one to bail out and I think we were at about 800 when I dove out the bomb bay. When I got on the ground, I found Pete and we started walking toward what we hoped would be our lines. We knew the general direction of our lines, but the heavy snow coming down prevented us from knowing what direction we were heading. After walking for a couple of hours, we rounded a grove of trees and walked into a German camp. Needless to say, we were taken prisoner and placed in a holding pen till the Germans could decide what to do with us. Pete kept washing the blood off my face with snow, and he really boosted my morale by telling me we would escape. That night we did try to escape, but Pete was killed by the guard and I was recaptured, blindfolded, and had my hands tied behind my back with rope. That was the way I stayed during the three months I was a prisoner."

"Did Pete suffer when he was shot?" Ellen wanted to know.

"I'm sure he did not, because it was so quick. I really don't think Pete knew what hit him." I continued. "Pete was one of my best friends, and when I was finally able to make my escape, I killed the guard that shot Pete by bringing the butt of his own rifle down on his head repeatedly before I left."

After that long saga of how their son was lost, we were all drained emotionally. Ellen suggested taking a drive along the shore.

Driving with all of the car windows opened allowed the salty breezes to engulf us. Paul took us to a large marina and showed me his five fishing cruisers. He said, "I have a captain for each boat and we are partners, sharing everything on a fifty-fifty basis. It's a good venture and, after the war is over, I plan to build my own marina." He then asked me, "What do you plan to do after the war is over, Bill?"

"I've decded on a military career. First of all, because I want to be sure I am all patched up. And second, because I love the military service and flying is in my blood. I feel that a strong military is necessary for our country because this will not be the last war in our lifetime."

"That is a very profound statement for a man as young as you to make, and I am in total agreement with you," Paul said.

Ellen had been very quiet during our drive and she finally said, "I think Pete would have felt the same way you do, Bill."

After spending three days with those wonderful parents of my friend, it was time for me to go back to my family. Both Ellen and Paul hugged me and told me how much my visit meant to them. They said I would always be welcome in their home.

I said goodbye to Ellen at the house because she said she didn't want people to see her cry in public. Paul took me to meet the station master at the train depot and showed me how I could get to Cincinnati from Port Arthur by taking the southern route. He even took the time to plan the trip for me, so I would have a minimum of train changes.

Paul tried to buy my ticket but I told him, "I really appreciate your offer, but this whole trip was something I just had to do myself."

He said, "I think maybe I understand, Bill."

We went to the car to get my B-4 bag, and Paul reached into the trunk and brought out a big jar of his famous shrimp sauce. I placed it in a side pocket of my B-4 bag.

The long trip back to Cincinnati was as comfortable as possible because Paul's friend, the station master, had reserved Pullman roomettes for me all the way home.

Once again I arrived at the Cincinnati Union Terminal and took a taxi to Hyde Park. Grandmother and Aunt Verna were sitting on the porch. I sat with them for a while, as they wanted to know all about the people I met on my trip. Verna told me I had had twenty-seven phone calls while I was gone, and they were all listed on the phone table.

I telephoned my sister but got no answer, so I telephoned Roberta.

"How was the graduation?" I asked.

"It was very formal and very impressive. Wish you could have been there."

"Me, too, but a big weight has gone from my shoulders after spending some time with the parents of two of my best friends."

Roberta said, "I know you must be very tired after such a long trip, but my mother and father are anxious to see our local hero. How about dinner at my house tomorrow night?"

"That sounds great, but knock off that hero stuff."

"Have it your way," she laughed, "but to your friends, you are our very own hero."

The next morning, while going down the list of phone numbers, I noticed one was from the Army Counterintelligence School in Montgomery, Alabama, so I called that number next. I was informed that my name had been selected to attend the seven-month counterintelligence officer's course that was to start on July 1 and that orders were being sent to my home address.

I was quite surprised. "Sergeant, I'm on a ninety-day R and R leave, and that will not be up until August 7."

"I'm sorry, Lieutenant, but a Colonel Ledoux sent a personal letter to the school commandant recommending you highly for the course because of your wartime experiences. I happen to know, Lieutenant, that you were picked over eighteen officers senior to you based on Colonel Ledoux's recommendation."

"I thank you for telling me that," I replied. "Sergeant, I'll report to the school at the appointed time."

It took me most of that day and the next to finish my phone calls. I went upstairs to shave, shower, and put on a clean uniform before going to Roberta's.

When I drove up in front of the house, her father, Robert, came to the curb to greet me with a hug. He told me how glad he was to see me looking so well after what I had been through. When we walked up on the porch, his wife, Ann, came out on the porch and hugged me like one of the family. The three of us sat on the porch, as Ann told me Roberta had a late hair appointment but should be back very soon. A short time later, she drove up and joined us on the porch.

When Roberta and her mother went into the house to finish getting dinner ready, Bob pulled out a couple of cigars and offered me one. I noticed they were cedar-wrapped Tampa Straights, and I told him about the wonderful people from New York that I had met in Tampa. After telling Bob about my experience of trying to buy a box of Tampa Diplomats, we both had a good laugh.

During a most enjoyable dinner, Bob and Ann both had questions about my experiences but Roberta spoke up and said, "Bill is just not comfortable talking about that at this time."

I told them, "I hope you understand."

"Of course we understand," replied Bob, "and when you are ready to talk about it we will be here to listen with much interest."

After dinner Roberta and I decided to go for a ride. I thanked her mother for a most enjoyable dinner. Bob said, "Come back anytime, Bill. Maybe we can take in a ballgame while you are on leave."

"I'd really enjoy that," I said. "It's been almost four years since I've seen the Reds play ball."

As we drove away from the house, I told Roberta, "My leave ends this weekend."

"I thought you had ninety days," she said.

"I thought so, too, but one of the calls I had while I was on my trip was from the Army telling me of my assignment to the Army Counterintelligence School in Alabama as a student. I am to start classes on July 1. It is a great career opportunity to be considered for an intelligence assignment, and one of my former commanding officers pushed through the appointment for me. I'll be leaving on Monday, and my grandmother doesn't even know." In order to cheer things up, I asked, "Where would you like to go tonight?"

"I don't care. Have you been to the Barn since you've been home?"

"Negative," I said.

"You fliers talk a funny language, don't you?"

"It's not a funny language to us because the purpose is brevity. That is important up in the air, when you are moving at over two hundred miles per hour. Some people do run it into the ground, though, and I try not to do that."

A good band was playing at the Barn and I was able to make it through three slow dances with my cane hanging on my arm. We were both surprised that we did not see any of our friends there because it was always a favorite spot. Of course, we were there on a Thursday and the place usually didn't start jumping until Friday night. The three dances really wore me out, so we departed early.

I took Roberta home to a house that was dark except for the hall light. I kissed her good night at the door and then barely made it home, because I was so sleepy.

I planned to sleep late in the morning but I was awakened at 8:00 when a Western Union boy propped his bicycle against the hedge and rang the doorbell to deliver a telegram to me. The wire advised me that the start of classes for the counterintelligence school and my reporting were moved up three days. Since I planned to drive to Alabama so I would have my car with me, that meant I would have to leave that day.

Verna was in the kitchen preparing breakfast and Grandmother soon came downstairs. I told them both about the telegram. Verna said, "Get all your dirty clothes together and I'll get them washed for you so you can start out with all clean clothes."

After breakfast, I telephoned Roberta and told her about

the change in my orders. She asked when we would see each other again.

"I still have over thirty days left on my R and R leave, but I don't know when or if I will get to use that," I told her. "I understand that particular school is not a snap course, and I will probably be burning a lot of the old midnight oil studying. However, I do know the Army closes down schools during the Christmas holidays. Let's plan on the Christmas holidays, and if I can get home earlier, I will."

Before I hung up the phone, Verna said, "Ask her to come over and have lunch with us." I did and Roberta was there within twenty minutes. I made a few more phone calls to friends and tried to call my sister again but still no answer. After lunch I packed my car, said goodbye to my family and my special girlfriend, and took off in my red Ford for the beginning of my new adventure as a career officer in the Army Air Forces.

My wartime adventures remained locked away in my mind and unrevealed for many years. My first departure from Cincinnati had been as a patriotic teenager going overseas to fight for his country. This departure, even though only three years later, I was leaving Cincinnati as a seasoned career officer in the Army Air Forces, embarking on a new adventure in the intelligence service of his country.

William L. Cramer, Jr.
Post World War II

1945–1946	1. Counterintelligence Course, Montgomery, Alabama.
1946–1947	1. Occupation Forces in Germany. Testified at the War Crimes Trials. 2. Air Intelligence Officer. European Air Transport Service, Weisbaden, Germany. 3. Base Intelligence Officer. Tulln Air Base, Vienna, Austria.
1947–1949	1. Provost Marshal. 4902nd Air Base Group, Kelly Field, Texas. 2. Student. Air Intelligence Officer Course, Photo Interpretation Officer Course, Radar Scope Photo Interpretation Course, Lowry Field, Denver, Colorado.
1949–1951	1. Wing Intelligence Officer. 307th Bomb Wing, McDill Air Force Base, Florida.
1951–1952	1. War Planning Council. Flak Intelligence Officer, Far East Air Forces, Yokada, Japan.
1952–1955	1. Escape and Evasion School Director. 91st Strategic Reconnaissance Wing, Columbus, Ohio.
1955–1956	1. Student. Office of Special Investigations Special Agents Academy. Georgetown University, School of Foreign Service.
1956–1960	1. Commander, OSI Detachment. Evreux Air Force Base, France. Deep Cover Agent, with another federal intelligence agency. Europe, Mid-East, Viet Nam.

1960–1962	1. Commander, OSI Detachment, Atlanta, Georgia.
1963	1. Retirement. After twenty-one years of continuous active duty, retired from the United States Air Force.
1963–1965	1. Department Manager. First National Bank, Memphis, Tennessee.
1965–1971	1. Manager. Pinkerton's National Detective Agency, Memphis, Tennessee.
1968–1969	1. Deputy Wing Commander. Civil Air Patrol (Auxiliary of the U.S. Air Force), Memphis, Tennessee.
1969–1971	1. Wing Commander. Civil Air Patrol, Memphis, Tennessee.
1971–1979	1. District Manager. Wells Fargo, Atlanta, Georgia, and Memphis, Tennessee.
	2. Inspector General. Southeast Region, Civil Air Patrol, Atlanta, Georgia.
1979–1981	1. Assistant Regional Manager. Pinkerton's, Dallas, Texas.
	2. Wing Inspector. Civil Air Patrol, Dallas, Texas.
1981–1984	1. Corporate Director of Investigations. Total Assets Protection, Inc., Arlington, Texas.
1984–1986	1. President. Cramer & Cramer Investigations, Bedford, Texas.
1986–	1. President. Cramer Intelligence Associates, Bedford, Texas.
	2. Inspector General. Southwest Region, Civil Air Patrol, Dallas, Texas.
	3. Writer and after-dinner speaker.

Captain – Wing Intelligence Officer

Major – OSI Commander – France

– La Pipe –

Intelligence agent en route to Sicily as a French businessman.

En route to Bulgaria as a French businessman.

In North Africa as a French tourist.

Lieutenant Colonel – Deputy Wing Commander

Colonel – Tennessee Wing Commander

Colonel Cramer – Inspector General, Southwest Region, Civil Air Patrol

Index

A

A-2 jackets, 35–36, 43, 117–118
Air Medal, 43, 44
American Embassy, 54
Annie (English friend), 66–69
Antwerp, Germany, 51
Apalachicola, 10
APCs, 39
Army Counterintelligence School, 144
Army General Classification Test, 2
AT-6, 7, 10
Avon River, 92

B

B-17, 14, 22, 26, 30, 31, 34–35, 39, 45, 57, 65, 71, 119, 137
B-17E, 38
B-17F, 49
B-17G, 77, 78, 79, 81, 82, 96
B-34, 7
Bailleaul, France, 116
Ball, Lieutenant Colonel, 65
Bangor, Maine, 32, 119
Barn, the, 126, 146
Battle of Britain, 93
Battle of the Bulge, 97, 142
Belgium underground, 111
Ben (friend at Spetchley), 90–91, 92, 94
Berlin, Germany, 39, 50, 60, 61
Bond Hill, 128
Bremen, Germany, 39
British Coastal Watch, 51–52
British Red Cross, 89, 91
Brooklyn, New York, 28
Brussels, Germany, 83
Buckeye Babe, 49
Buckley Field (Denver, CO), 6, 23
Burns, Colonel, 77, 97, 117–118

C

C-47, 30
C-54, 35
Cadet Training Program, 4, 6, 10, 31, 45, 62
Caen, France, 63
Calais, France, 51, 116
Carmichael, Hoagy, 23
Chuck (navigator), 62–63
Church Army Canteen, 37
Cincinnati, Ohio, 16, 67, 121
Claude (underground agent), 111–113
Cologne, Germany, 81, 83
Combat America, 37
County Cork, Ireland, 67
Coventry, England, 93
Cramer, Betty Jane, 2
  Margaret Boulware, 2, 122, 124, 130, 132, 144, 146
  Russell Elton, 122–124
  Virginia, 127, 129
  Cramer, William L., Jr.: as armour/gunner, 10; basic training, 3–4; battlefield

commission of, 46–47; bombardier training, 6–9, 31, 45–46; childhood, 2; combat crew training, 14–28; in crash landings, 19, 34–35, 51, 69–71, 74, 86–87; enlists in Army Air Corps, 1; escapes from Germans, 110; gunnery training, 10–13; helped by underground, 111–116; medals awarded to, 43, 44, 88, 117, 122; as prisoner of war, 101–110; promoted to sgt., 4, staff sgt., 11, 2nd lieut., 46; radar/navigation training, 45, 78; second combat tour of, 85; uses "La Pipe" code name, 114; wings authorized to, 48
William L., Sr., 2, 122, 124, 127, 129
Cramer Furniture Manufacturing Company, 31

D

D-Day, 63–64
Deke (bombardier), 58–59
Diaz, Hoke, 23–25
Distinguished Flying Cross, 88
Drew Field, 26, 27–28
Duke, 81–82
Dunmire, Hershel, 49
Dusseldorf, Germany, 51

E

Easton, Verna Cramer, 122, 124, 130, 132, 144, 146
8th Air Force, 11, 13, 14, 89
Emden, Germany, 39
English Channel, 98

F

FFI (French underground), 113
Fishburne, Maj. Paul, 56, 75, 77–78
511th Bomb Squadron, 91
509th Bomb Squadron, 75, 91
flight officer rating, 8
Floridian Hotel, 23, 28
Flying Evaluation Board, 35
Fort Wright, 37
Fountain Square, 126
Fred (ball turret gunner), 54–55
Frisches, 130
Fritz, Cpl. Al, 8–9
Ft. Thomas, 2
FW 190s, 39, 49, 77, 79

G

Gable, Clark, 11–13, 37–38, 62
Galveston, Texas, 142
Georgia Lee, 34
German 88s, 50
German Air Force, 107
Gestapo, 111
Gold Star Flag, 122, 124
Goose Bay, Labrador, 32

H

Hagen, Ellen, 140–144
Paul, 140–144
Pete, 53–56, 97, 101–104, 112, 117, 127, 140–144
Hamburg, Germany, 65, 85
Hamlet, 91, 94
Hamm, Germany, 53
Hanchett, Cpl. Ruff, 29
Hannover, Germany, 51
Hava-Tampa Cigar Company, 25
Helen (nurse), 116–117, 118–119
Henry (English coal miner), 57–58
Hope Diamond, 25
Houston, Texas, 26, 139
Howard, Lt. Don, 29
Hughes High School, 131
Hunter Field (Savannah, GA), 30
Hyde Park (Cincinnati), 58, 67, 121, 125
Hythe, England, 116

I

Idlewild Restaurant, 59
IG Farbenin chemical plant, 40

J

Jack (Jean's brother), 19–20, 133
Jean (friend of Bill Cramer), 16, 17, 19, 21, 132–133
Joanna (Red Cross hostess), 89, 90–91, 92, 94
Joe (navigator), 99–100
Jones, Cpl. Bud, 28, 29
Josh (English coal miner), 57–58, 66–69

K

Kansas City, Kansas, 132
Kassel, Germany, 52, 82
Keesler Field, Mississippi, 2

Ken (navigator), 73
Kevin (navigator), 79–80
Kiel, Germany, 61
King George (footman), 91–93, 94–95
King Lear, 90
King's Cliff, 61, 98

L
La Pipe (underground agent), 114–116
Le Bourget airfield, 65
Ledoux, Maj. Elzia, 44–46, 48, 71, 88–89, 145
Leipzig, Germany, 69, 71
Lille, France, 114
Lombard, Carole, 37
London, England, 54, 57, 58, 66
Ludwigshafen, Germany, 40, 78
Luftwaffe, 79

M
McDill Field, 27
McFarlin, Lt. Charlie (Mac), 27, 29, 32–33, 40
McIntyre, Andy, 11–13, 37
Magdeburg, Germany, 51, 82
Marie (underground agent), 111–113
Mark (English friend), 66–69
Me 109s, 39, 49, 77, 79
Meents, Johnny, 1, 124–125, 127, 130
MENSA, 2
Merseburg, Germany, 61, 69, 77
Mick (English coal miner), 57–58
Miller, Glenn, 16, 43
Min (English friend), 66–69
Molesworth Airfield, 74, 77
Montgomery, Alabama, 144
Moore, Cpl. Amos, 26–27, 29, 32, 39
  Jake, 26
Munich, Germany, 71–72
Munster, Germay, 51

N
Norden bombsight, 7, 31, 33, 35, 64
Nurnburg, Germany, 82
Nye, T/Sgt., 23

O
100th Bomb Group, 42
Oundle, England, 52, 98
Overseas Training Unit, 14

P
Paddington Station, 57
Paris, France, 78
Pearl Harbor, 25
Pearson, Cpl. Thor, 29
Peenemunde, 75
Peterborough, England, 54, 57, 59
Piccadilly Circus, 57
Plant Park, 21, 22, 31
Plauen, Germany, 78
Polebrook Air Base, 35, 45, 50, 52, 61, 75, 78, 83, 86
Politz, Germany, 83
Port Arthur, Texas, 127, 139
Potsdam, Germany, 51
Preswick, Scotland, 119
Purple Cow, 16, 126
Purple Heart Medal, 88, 117, 122

Q
Quinn, Lt. Paul, 22–23, 25, 26–28, 29, 30–35, 38, 40, 43, 44, 46

R
RAF, 54, 58, 93, 94
RAF Hawkinge, 45, 51, 53, 78
RCAF, 54, 55
Red Cross, 118, 122
Red Cross Club, 54, 55, 58
Reykjavik, Iceland, 33–34
Rheims, France, 56
Rialto Theater, 58
Richardson, Maj. Frank, 77, 84, 86, 88–89, 117–118
Roberta (friend of Bill Cramer), 128–129, 130–131, 144, 145–146, 146–147
Robinson, Bob, 133–138
  Irene, 134–136, 137–139
  Mary, 133, 134–138
  Robbie, 56–57, 59, 60, 61, 62–63, 66, 71, 72, 75, 76, 80, 83, 84, 85, 87–88, 118, 127, 133–134, 136–137
Romig, Colonel, 50
Roper, Major, 72, 76

Rosa (underground agent), 114
Rose and Crown pub, 52, 98
Royal Scot, 54, 57, 59, 119
Rueban, Corporal, 3–4
Ruhr Valley, 76
Runte, George, 2, 125–127, 128

S
Saarbrucken, Germany, 78
Saint Hubert, Belgium, 111
St. Omer, France, 116
Salina, Kansas, 127, 132, 135–136
Schweinfurt, Germany, 49, 54, 76
Senk, Cpl. Lee, 29, 38
Settle, Georgia Lee, 34, 35
Shakespeare Memorial Theater, 90, 94–95
Silver Star, 117, 120
Sioux City Army Air Base, 14, 15
Sioux City, Iowa, 16, 132
Spetchley Park Manor, 88, 89–90, 95
SS troops, 111
Stewart, Jimmy, 119
Straits of Dover, 116
Stratford-upon-Avon, 88, 90

T
Tampa Diplomats, 24, 25, 145
Tampa Nuggets, 23, 25
Tee-Pee, 135
351st Bomb Group, 37, 42, 49, 75, 81, 117
303rd Bomb Group, 74
303rd General Hospital, 40, 42, 87, 116
Traylor, Bob, 59–60
Tyndall Field (Panama City, FL), 9, 10, 31

U
underground organization, 111–116
University of Cincinnati, 125, 128
University Club, 128, 130
University of Kansas, 135
USO Club, 16

V
V.K.F. ball-bearing plant, 76
V-1 rockets, 55, 75
V-2 rockets, 75

W
War Bond tour, 84, 85
War Department, 122, 124
Wesel, Germany, 39
White Cliffs of Dover, 51
Wilhelmshaven, Germany, 38
Wilhurst Saddle Club, 25
Withrow High School, 34
Worchester, England, 89
World War I, 17, 125